AQA Accounting

Exclusively endorsed by AQA

AS

D0785747

David Austen

Peter Hailstone

Nelson Thornes

First published in 2008, this edition published in 2012 by:
Nelson Thornes Ltd
Delta Place
27 Bath Road
CHELTENHAM
GL53 7TH
United Kingdom

12 13 14 15 16 / 10 9 8 7 6 5 4 3 2 1

A catalogue record for this book is available from the British Library

ISBN 978 1 4085 1557 0

Cover photograph by Alamy

Page make-up by Fakenham Photosetting, Norfolk

Printed in China by 1010 Printing International Ltd

Acknowledgements
Photo p.v Getty Images

Contents

Contents 2011004 8 CO

AQA introduction

Nelson Thornes has worked in partnership with AQA to ensure this book offers you the best support for your A Level course.

This book has been approved by senior AQA examiners so you can feel assured that it closely matches the specification for this subject and provides you with everything you need to prepare successfully for your exams.

How to use this book

This book covers the specification for your course and is arranged in a sequence approved by AQA.

The book content is divided into chapters and topics that match the AQA Accounting specification for Units 1 and 2 – Financial Accounting and Financial and Management Accounting. Chapters 1–4 cover Unit 1 and Chapters 5–11 cover Unit 2.

The features in this book include:

Learning objectives

At the beginning of each chapter and topic you will find a list of learning objectives that contain targets linked to the requirements of the specification.

Key terms

Terms that you will need to be able to define and understand.

Case study

An overarching business scenario, to be used throughout a topic or chapter.

Illustration

A worked example that will show you how to go through a particular accounting skill.

Activity

Suggestions for practical investigations you can carry out, these will help you to test your knowledge and understanding

Background knowledge

An extension to the main text that will provide you with added bits of useful knowledge.

Links

This highlights any areas where topics relate to another part of this book, or to the A2 specification.

AQA Examiner's tip

Hints from AQA examiners to help you with your study and to prepare for your exam.

AQA Examination-style questions

Questions in the style that you can expect in your exam appear at the end of each topic and chapter.

AQA examination questions are reproduced by permission of the Assessment and Qualifications Alliance.

Learning outcomes

A bulleted list at the end of each topic or chapter summarising the content in an easy-to-follow way.

Web links in the book

As Nelson Thornes is not responsible for third party content online, there may be some changes to this material that are beyond our control. In order for us to ensure that the links referred to in the book are as up-to-date and stable as possible, the websites are usually homepages with supporting instructions on how to reach the relevant pages if necessary.

Please let us know at **kerboodle@nelsonthornes.com** if you find a link that doesn't work and we will do our best to redirect the link, or to find an alternative site. if you find a link that doesn't work and we will do our best to correct this at reprint, or to list an alternative site.

Financial accounting

Chapters in this unit:

Introduction to Unit 1

Unit 1 is designed as the foundation of the course covering double entry procedures as applied to the accounting systems of sole traders, the verification of accounting records and the preparation of income statements and statements of financial position (balance sheets). The lessons learned in this unit will form the solid foundations to be built on in your remaining studies.

The chapters in this section of the book follow the four sections of the specification:

As an introduction to the subject, **Chapter 1** looks at the reasons for keeping accounting records and the interests that stakeholders will have in these records.

Assessment could be based on the benefits to a business of maintaining accurate financial records or on identifying stakeholders and stating their particular interests in the accounting records.

Chapter 2 introduces the important rules of double entry bookkeeping that will be essential to all of your future studies in accounting and develops the necessary skills to enable students to identify source documents and account for these in the subsidiary books. Each subsidiary book is described in detail as is the process of posting from subsidiary books to the ledger system.

Candidates are expected to understand the different stages as a transaction passes through the accounting system, enabling them to accurately write up and close off day books, ledger accounts and cash books. In addition, candidates should be prepared for questions requiring them to identify the source document and subsidiary books that would be relevant to particular transactions.

Having processed transactions through the ledger system, **Chapter 3** details the important aspects of verification of the records by means of trial balance, bank reconciliation statements and sales and purchase ledger control accounts. In addition, the chapter addresses the issue of errors and error correction by means of the suspense account, together with assessing the effect that errors may have on profit calculations.

This section of the specification requires that candidates are able to understand the purpose and limitations of trial balances, control accounts and bank reconciliation statements as well as being able to prepare them. Candidates will be expected to identify different types of error, to assess what effect, if any, the error would have on profit calculations and to process corrections using a suspense account.

The final **Chapter 4** in Unit 1 builds on the knowledge acquired in earlier chapters and enables students to prepare the end-of-year financial statements of a sole trader from a trial balance. The chapter introduces the concept of simple adjustments to both the end-of-year financial statements and the ledger accounts in the form of expense prepayments, accruals and bad debts. Students will also learn how to adjust the financial statements for depreciation using the straight-line method.

Assessment may involve the preparation of all, or part of a set of financial statements involving closing adjustments. Candidates should be familiar with all presentational aspects of financial statements and be prepared to make the necessary amendments to an incorrect statement of financial position (balance sheet).

Your examination will balance computational questions requiring, for example, the preparation of financial statements, control accounts or ledger accounts with written topics requiring you to identify or explain various accounting techniques or teminology.

In order to be successful in your examination, you must be very confident in your knowledge of the basic principles of double entry bookkeeping. This will enable you to confidently identify the debits and credits in a trial balance and correctly transfer these items into the financial statements. You may be presented with an incorrect trial balance or statement of financial position (balance sheet) and be required to prepare corrected versions of these. Once again, the key to this type of question is a sound knowledge of double entry principles.

Throughout the examination, candidates should be aware that they will be rewarded for good presentational skills and also that it is in their own interests to show workings wherever relevant.

1 Purposes of accounting

In this chapter you will learn:

- the reasons for keeping accounting records
- the benefits that arise for the owners of a business and other stakeholders.

All businesses should keep accurate and up-to-date accounting records. These help the owners of the business to manage their affairs properly and enable outside stakeholders to assess how well the business is performing. This enables those stakeholders to safeguard their own interests. In this chapter you will learn the reasons why a business should keep these accounting records and also who these outside stakeholders are and what benefits they will gain from the accounts. Throughout your AS Level studies you should remember these reasons because they will help you understand the purpose of the various techniques you are going to study.

Background knowledge

In practice, most businesses now keep their accounting records on computers, but computerised systems simply undertake all of the manual processes electronically. The processes we are studying for this unit are all manual.

Key terms

Profit: the amount by which income exceeds the costs of running a business in a trading period.

Income statement: a record in two sections: showing a business's gross profit based on comparing sales with the cost of sales; and a business's profit or loss, based on gross profit less running costs.

Statement of financial position (balance sheet): a statement detailing all of the assets and liabilities of a business.

Stakeholders: individuals or organisations that have an interest (sometimes financial) in the organisation.

What are the reasons for keeping accounting records?

The practice of keeping accounting records goes back many thousands of years. In days gone by, traders would keep records of the money they spent and the money they received in order to see whether or not they had made a **profit**.

The same principles apply today, but clearly the scale and complexity of the accounting requirements has changed considerably as the scale and complexity of business has changed.

So, what are the reasons for keeping accounting records and the benefits to the owner of a business?

Recording and reporting what has happened in the past

All businesses need to be able to assess whether the business is profitable. Recording historic **income** and **expenditure**, and producing an **income statement**, enables this to be done.

Similarly, all businesses need to be able to assess whether they are solvent (i.e. do they have sufficient assets to pay all of their liabilities). Producing a **statement of financial position (balance sheet)** enables this to be done.

These reports enable **stakeholders** to be kept informed.

Forecasting for the future

Based on what has happened historically, owners are able to forecast what they anticipate will happen in the future, in the form of cash budgets or *projected* income statements and statements of financial position.

Case study

Brian

Brian started his business as a baker three years ago and the business is expanding quickly. He has approached his bank for a loan to finance the expansion. And the bank has asked to see projected figures for the next year.

Link

For more information on cash budgets, see Chapter 10, page 157–9.

Link

For more information on projected income statements, see A2 Module 4.

Key terms

Income: the value of resources received and receivable in the course of business.

Expenditure: the value of resources used by the business in acquiring goods and services.

Activity

Accounting information

Andrew has started a business selling car parts. List the information you would expect Andrew to keep records of.

Background knowledge

The accounts of a business will inform third parties of the performance of a business. These third parties, the stakeholders, need this information to make judgements about the business for various reasons.

Key terms

Liquidity: the ability of a business to access sufficient cash resources to pay its short-term liabilities.

Link

For more information on liquidity, see Chapter 9, page 147.

By looking at the trends of business for the past 12 months and assessing the business that he knows he has in the coming months, Brian will be able to prepare a projected income statement to forecast the profit he will make, a projected statement of financial position (balance sheet) to forecast the condition of his business in the future and a cash budget to determine whether he will have a shortfall of cash in the coming months. This will enable Brian to identify the amount of finance he requires and the bank to ascertain whether Brian's business is a safe proposition as a borrower.

Monitoring and control

Accurate accounting records enable owners and managers to monitor what has actually happened in the business, compare this with what was forecast to happen and then take corrective action when necessary.

A legal requirement

Businesses have a legal requirement to maintain complete and accurate accounting records, principally to enable HM Revenue and Customs to collect all amounts due in respect of taxes.

Benefits to the stakeholders of a business

The individuals and organisations that have an interest in the accounts of a business are known as the stakeholders. They each have reasons for needing to know how safe and profitable the business is.

Owners

The owners of a business need to know whether the business is profitable and also to assess the **liquidity** of the business. Is the business generating sufficient cash to pay its liabilities in a timely fashion?

Managers

To enable managers to make decisions regarding the policies of the business, to plan for the future and to exercise control over the business. Without access to the financial statements, managers may inadvertently make decisions that are either not in the best interests of the company or are not practical in the light of resources that are available to them.

Suppliers

To assess whether the business is able to pay for the goods and services supplied according to the agreed terms.

Customers

To assess the continued viability of the business to meet their needs. In other words, will the business be able to supply goods ordered?

Providers of finance

Lenders, for example banks, finance companies, etc., need to assess whether the business can continue to meet its obligations to repay borrowings together with interest due on those borrowings.

Employees

To assess whether the business is able to continue trading and therefore continue to provide employment and pay wages that are due.

Government

To assess how much income tax and value added tax is due from the business.

Competitors

To assess how well their own business is performing in comparison. Does the competitor have higher sales, better profitability, etc.? This will enable competitors to identify problems in their own business and attempt to rectify them.

Potential investors

To assess the viability of investment in the business.

Local community

To assess the impact of the business on local community issues and the environment.

Case study

Recycle plc

Recycle plc is a multinational company with large plants throughout the world. The company has applied for planning permission to build a waste recycling plant on the outskirts of a village in Cornwall. The village is in an area of great natural beauty and relies very heavily on the tourist industry throughout the year. The local residents would be concerned as to the impact this would have on the local environment, on wildlife, on the business that tourists bring to the area and generally on the quality of their own lives.

Activity

Petroco

Petroco, a leading international petrochemical company has applied for planning permission for a processing plant on the outskirts of Hornbeach, a seaside town on the south coast of England. The company has organised a public meeting to gauge local opinion.

Detail the issues that are likely to be raised at the meeting.

AQA Examiner's tip

In question 1, be specific. Take each statement in turn and identify its purpose.

Learning outcomes

As a result of studying this chapter, you should now be able to:

- identify the reasons for keeping accounting records
- identify the main 'stakeholders' of a business
- identify the main reasons why the stakeholders of a business have an interest in the financial statements

AQA Examination Style Questions

1   Explain how a sole trader benefits from keeping accounting records.

2   Kenny is a sole trader. He owns a chain of five coffee bars located in the suburbs of a city in the Midlands. Identify two internal and three external stakeholders and describe their interest in Kenny's business.

The basic principles of double entry bookkeeping are an essential skill that will be developed throughout your accounting course. The rules of double entry bookkeeping have been in existence for many centuries and most of the techniques and procedures you are going to learn rely very heavily on you having a good understanding of these rules.

This chapter will introduce you to the basic mechanics of double entry bookkeeping and introduce a number of terms that need to be remembered because they will occur throughout the course.

You will be introduced to the stages in the accounting process that are to be studied throughout this unit and will learn how to process a transaction from the beginning as a source document, through subsidiary books into the ledger system.

As you progress through your studies you will see that these basic principles remain unaltered and that all of the accounting techniques that you learn follow the same set of rules.

1 Source documents and double entry bookkeeping

In this topic you will learn:

- the basic mechanics of double entry bookkeeping
- how to recognise different source documents.

Double entry bookkeeping

All businesses must record transactions in their books of account. Double entry bookkeeping recognises that every transaction has a **dual aspect.** In other words, two accounts are affected and both sides of a transaction must be accounted for, the debit entry and the credit entry.

Each account has two sides – the **DEBIT** (on the left-hand side) and the **CREDIT** (on the right-hand side). These accounts are known as **T ACCOUNTS** and are set out in Figure 2.1.

The basic rule of double entry bookkeeping is that for every debit there must always be equal and corresponding credit(s).

When deciding which account to debit and which account to credit, you may find it helpful to recall the mnemonic '**DEAD CLIC**' (Fig. 2.2).

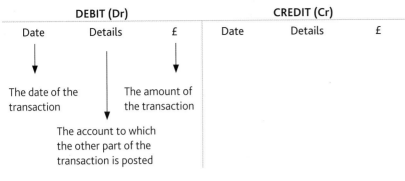

Figure 2.1 *T Accounts*

DEBIT (Dr)	CREDIT (Cr)
Expenditure	Liabilities
Assets	Income
Drawings	Capital

Figure 2.2 *DEAD CLIC*

The accounting equation

One of the most important fundamental principles in accounting is the accounting equation. This states that:

Assets – Liabilities = Capital

Assets are the resources that a business owns and uses to run the business and to produce and sell goods and services. Examples of assets are machinery, premises, inventory and cash.

Liabilities are amounts that the business owes to third parties, for example amounts owed to suppliers, bank overdrafts, loans, etc.

Capital is the investment in the business made by the owner. It comprises the initial investment plus profits made, less profits withdrawn by the owner in the form of **drawings**.

If you wish to increase the value of an account with a debit balance or reduce the value of an account with a credit balance, then that account should be debited.

If you wish to increase the value of an account with a credit balance or reduce the value of an account with a debit balance, then that account should be credited.

Illustration

Examples of debit and credit entries

1 Andrew purchases new machinery for his business paying £900 by cheque.

Key terms

DEAD CLIC: a mnemonic to help remember the rules of Debit and Credit
Debit
Expenditure
Assets
Drawings
Credit
Liabilities
Income
Capital.

Assets: resources that are available for use by the business.

Liabilities: monies owed by the business.

Capital: resources (cash or other assets) introduced by the owner to run the business.

Drawings: funds withdrawn from the business by the owner for personal use.

Background knowledge

The accounting equation is a very important principle. You should remember this throughout your studies in accounting as it will apply to every set of financial statements you prepare.

Case study

Norman's Books

Norman's Books was set up in July 2011 by Harry Norman. He sells books from a rented shop in Canterbury.

AQA Examiner's tip

Take each of the above transactions in turn and decide which two accounts are affected and what effect the transaction will have on those accounts. It will help if you undertake this exercise by reference to the mnemonic 'DEAD CLIC'.

Key terms

Payables: amounts owed to suppliers, who are sometimes referred to as 'creditors'.

Receivables: amounts owed by customers, who are sometimes referred to as 'debtors'.

Debit	Credit	Explanation
Machinery		New machinery is an asset, so the value of the asset of machinery increases by £900
Bank		The value of the asset of cash in the bank decreases by £900

2 Brian sells goods for £400 cash.

Debit	Credit	Explanation
Cash		Cash is an asset, so the value of cash increases by £400
Sales		At the same time, income increases by £400

3 Christine pays £800 rent by cheque.

Debit	Credit	Explanation
Rent		Expenditure is a debit
Bank		Cash at bank is an asset, so the value of cash at bank reduces by £800

Illustration

How to detail double entry

Norman's Books sells books. The following transactions were recorded in first week of trading.

1 July	Introduced capital of £10,000 into the bank account.
2 July	Purchased a delivery van for £2,500 paying by cheque.
3 July	Purchased books for resale on credit from Bookworm Ltd for £4,300.
3 July	Sold books for £540. Customer paid by cheque.
3 July	Sold books for £2,280 on credit to Daly Bookshops.
4 July	Purchased books for resale £580 paying by cheque.
6 July	Paid rent by cheque £1,200.
7 July	Paid cheque for £600 for drawings.

Required

Detail the double entry for each of the above transactions.

Date	Solution	Explanation
1 July	Dr Cash at bank	Cash at bank is an asset and it increases by £10,000.
	Cr Capital	Capital is the cash introduced into the business and this increases the balance of capital.
2 July	Dr Delivery van	Delivery van is an asset and this increases with the purchase.
	Cr Cash at bank	Cash at bank is also an asset, but this decreases when the van is paid for.
3 July	Dr Purchases	Purchases are expenditure for the business and purchases increase.
	Cr Payables	Payables are a liability (a credit) and these also increase.
3 July	Dr Cash at bank	Cash at bank is an asset and it increases by £540.
	Cr Sales	Sales are income (a credit) and these also increase by £540.

3 July	Dr Receivables	Receivables are assets, money owed to the business, and these increase.
	Cr Sales	Sales are income (a credit) and these also increase.
4 July	Dr Purchases	Purchases are expenditure for the business and purchases increase.
	Cr Cash at bank	Cash at bank is also an asset, but this decreases when the books are paid for.
6 July	Dr Rent	Rent is expenditure for the business and the charge for rent increases.
	Cr Cash at bank	Cash at bank is also an asset, but this decreases when the rent is paid.
7 July	Dr Drawings	Drawings are expenditure by the business and these increase.
	Cr Cash at bank	Cash at bank is an asset and this decreases when the cheque for drawings is paid.

Stages in the accounting process

The flow chart in Figure 2.3 shows the stages in the accounting process following a transaction through the records.

■ The role of different source documents

Invoices

The seller of goods or services provides an **invoice** for the buyer. This invoice will detail the following information:

- ■ *Addresses* – the supplier's address, the customer's address and the delivery address (if different).
- ■ *Dates* – the order date and the delivery date.
- ■ *Reference* – a unique invoice number will be present, together with the customer's order number.
- ■ *Description* of the goods or services supplied.
- ■ *Value* – the total amount owed by the customer.
- ■ *Terms* – when the invoice is due for payment and any discount that is available to the customer.

The invoice informs the buyer how much is being paid for the goods or services.

Credit notes

Credit notes are sent from the supplier to the customer when an adjustment to the amount owed is required. This may for example, be due to a calculation error, an incorrect delivery, damage to the goods, returned goods or goods lost in transit.

The details to be included on a credit note are identical to those found on an invoice.

The credit note informs the buyer how much has been deducted from the amount owed to the supplier.

Cheque counterfoils

When a cheque is written, the details are recorded on the **cheque counterfoil** and this becomes the source document.

Source documents

Invoices, credit notes, cheque counterfoils, paying-in slip counterfoils, cash receipts, till rolls, information from bank statements

↓

Books of original entry

General journal, day books, cash book

↓

Ledgers

Sales ledger, purchase ledger, general ledger (nominal ledger)

↓

Trial balance

Extracted from the general ledger

↓

Financial statements

Income statement, statement of financial position (balance sheet)

Figure 2.3 *Accounting process*

The details to be recorded are:

- the date of the cheque
- the payee (the person the cheque is made payable to)
- the amount of the cheque
- each cheque has a unique sequential number and this must be included when the details are transferred into the accounting records.

Paying-in slip counterfoils

When cash or cheques are paid into the bank, the details are recorded on the **paying-in slip counterfoil** and this becomes the source document.

The details to be recorded are:

- the date of the paying-in
- the drawers of cheques (the persons paying the organisation) or the source of cash banked
- the amount of the cheques/cash banked.

Cash receipts and till rolls

When cash or cheques are received by a business, a **cash receipt** will be issued. This receipt may take the form of a till roll or alternatively may be a hand-written receipt. The duplicate copies of these receipts form the source document for cash and cheque receipts.

Information from bank statements

Payments and receipts may be debited or credited directly through the bank account. In these circumstances the **bank statement** itself becomes the source document for:

- **Direct debits.** Where authority is granted by the business to a third party (for example a supplier of goods or services) for fixed or variable payments to be made at the request of that third party.
- **Standing orders.** Where a fixed payment is made at regular intervals by the bank on the instructions of the business.
- **Bank interest and charges.** Where the bank processes its charge to the business for maintenance of the bank account or the interest on funds borrowed or invested.
- **Credit transfers.** Where money has been paid direct into the bank account of the business by a third party.
- **BACS (Bankers' Automated Clearing Service).** A computerised payment transfer system which is often used by businesses to pay wages, salaries, trade payables, etc.

Other key documents

Delivery note

A document detailing the goods that have been delivered by the supplier. This should be signed by the recipient and a copy returned to the supplier as proof of delivery.

Purchase order

A document raised by the purchasing department used to place an order with a supplier.

Remittance advice

A document sent with a payment advising the recipient which invoices, etc. are being paid.

Statement of account

A document sent to a customer detailing all recent transactions and informing them of the total amount outstanding.

■ Activity

Source documents

1 Explain the purpose of source documents.

2 Identify the source document that would provide information to enter in the accounting records in each of the following cases.

Transaction	Source document
Cash paid into the bank.	
Goods purchased on credit from a supplier.	
Credit for goods returned from a customer.	
Cheque paid to a supplier.	
Credit transfer receipt from a customer.	
Goods sold to a customer on credit.	

Learning outcomes

As a result of studying this topic, you should now be able to:

■ recognise the source documents and identify their purpose

■ understand the operation of double entry bookkeeping principles

■ account for basic cash and cheque transactions in a double entry bookkeeping system

■ Key terms

Bank statement: a printout issued by the bank detailing all receipts into the account, payments out of the account and a running balance.

Direct debit: where authority is granted by the business to a third party for fixed or variable payments to be made at the request of that third party.

Standing order: where a fixed payment is made at regular intervals by the bank on the instructions of the business.

Delivery note: a document detailing the goods that have been delivered by the supplier.

Purchase order: a document used to place an order with a supplier.

Remittance advice: a document sent with a payment, advising the recipient which invoices, etc. are being paid.

Statement of account: a document sent to a customer detailing all recent transactions and informing them of the total amount outstanding.

 Examination Style Questions

1 Complete the following table identifying the source document and double-entry required for each transaction.

Transaction	Source document	Account to be debited	Account to be credited
Purchased goods on credit from EDX Ltd			
Paid cash into business's bank account			
Paid office expenses by cheque			
Returns goods purchased on credit from EDX Ltd			
Bank deducted charges for the month			

2   Subsidiary books

In this topic you will learn:

- how to account for source documents in the subsidiary books.

Background knowledge

The subsidiary books are sometimes referred to as the books of prime entry – the first point of entry into the records of the business.

Key terms

Sales day book: book of original entry recording credit sales invoices.

General ledger: a ledger containing all impersonal accounts (those accounts that are not customers or suppliers).

Background knowledge

The subsidiary books are where transactions are recorded from the source documents described in Topic 1. The main books are as follows.

- Sales day book
- Sales returns day book
- Purchases returns day book
- Purchases returns day book
- Cash book
- Journal

Sales day book

The **sales day book** is simply a list of all credit sales transactions. Depending on the volume of transactions, the sales day book will be totalled daily, weekly or monthly. The usual layout for the sales day book is as follows:

Date	Customer	Total (£)
1 May	ABC Ltd	176.25
2 May	DEF Ltd	258.50
		434.75

Figure 2.4 *Sales day book*

Note

The individual total of the invoice will be posted to the debit of the customer's account in the sales ledger. The individual customer accounts in the sales ledger form part of the double entry system. The double entry is completed by posting the total amount to Sales in the **general ledger**.

The double entry postings in the above sales day book example are:

DEBIT ABC Ltd £176.25						
DEBIT DEF Ltd £258.50						
CREDIT Sales account £434.75						

Dr			Sales account			Cr
Date	Details	£	Date	Details	£
			2 May	Sales day book	434.75

Figure 2.5 *Double entry postings*

The customers' accounts in the sales ledger will appear as follows (see Figure 2.6), reflecting the amount owed (receivables) by these two companies.

Dr		ABC Ltd			Cr
Date	Details	£	Date	Details	£
1 May	Sales day book	176.25			

Dr		DEF Ltd			Cr
Date	Details	£	Date	Details	£
2 May	Sales day book	258.50			

Figure 2.6 *Customer accounts*

Sales returns day book

The **sales returns day book** is a list of all credit notes issued to customers. The usual layout for the sales returns day book is identical to the sales day book shown above. The individual total of the credit note will be posted this time to the CREDIT of the customer's account in the sales ledger and the total amount of credit notes will be posted to the DEBIT of Sales Returns account in the general ledger.

Key terms

Sales returns day book: book of original entry recording sales credit notes.

Purchases day book

The **purchases day book** is a list of all supplier invoices received in respect of credit transactions. As is the case with the sales day book, depending on the volume of transactions, this will also be totalled daily, weekly or monthly. The usual layout for the purchases day book is identical to the sales day book.

Background knowledge

Sales returns are often referred to as returns inwards.

Purchases Day Book		
Date	**Supplier**	**Total (£)**
1 June	PQR Ltd	98.70
2 June	STU Ltd	705.00
		803.70

Figure 2.7 *Purchases day book*

Note

The individual total of the invoice will this time be posted to the credit of the supplier's account in the purchases ledger. The individual supplier accounts in the purchases ledger form part of the double entry system. The double entry (see Figure 2.8) is completed by posting the total amount to Purchases in the general ledger.

The double entry postings in the above example are:					
DEBIT Purchases £803.70					
CREDIT PQR Ltd £98.70					
CREDIT STU Ltd £705.00					
Dr			**Purchases account**		**Cr**
Date	**Details**	**£**	**Date**	**Details**	**£**
2 June	Purchases day book	803.70			

Figure 2.8 *Double entry postings*

The suppliers' accounts in the sales ledger will now appear as follows, reflecting the amount owing (payables) to these two companies.

Dr			PQR Ltd			Cr
Date	Details	£	Date	Details		£
			1 June	Purchases day book		98.70

Dr			STU Ltd			Cr
Date	Details	£	Date	Details		£
			2 June	Purchases day book		705.00

Figure 2.9 *Supplier's accounts in the purchases ledger*

Purchases returns day book

The **purchases returns day book** is a list of all credit notes received from suppliers. The usual layout for the purchases returns day book is identical to the purchases day book shown above. The individual total of the credit note will be posted this time to the DEBIT of the supplier's account in the purchases ledger and the total amount of credit notes will be posted to the CREDIT of Purchases Returns account in the general ledger.

Analysed sales/purchases day book

An analysed day book (see Figure 2.10) would be used when the organisation required more analysis of their **sales** or **purchases**. This analysis could be for different products, different expense headings, different locations, etc. The double entry process is identical to that employed with a traditional day book, though postings of the analysed columns would be into different accounts in the general ledger dependent upon the analysis.

Date	Supplier	Total (£)	Purchases	Rent and rates	Advertising	Office costs	Other expenses

Figure 2.10 *Purchase day book*

Sales Day Book

Date	Customer		Total (£)

Purchases Day Book

Date	Supplier		Total (£)

Sales Returns Day Book

Date	Customer		Total (£)

Purchases Returns Day Book

Date	Supplier		Total (£)

Cash book

The cash book records all cash and bank transactions, together with details of discount allowed and discount received.

Whilst there are a variety of acceptable formats for a cash book (including analysed), the most common presentation is as follows:

Dr					Cash Book					Cr
Date	Details	Discount allowed	Cash	Bank	Date	Details received	Discount	Cash	Bank	

Figure 2.11 *Cash book*

The following table will help you remember into which side of the cash book data is to be entered.

Table 2.1 *Cash book data*

Cash columns	
Debit	Credit
Opening balance b/d – cash in hand	
Cash received	Cash paid
Cheque drawn for cash	
	Closing balance c/d – cash in hand

Bank columns	
Debit	Credit
Opening balance b/d – cash in bank	Opening balance – bank overdraft
Cheques received	Cheques paid
Bank interest received	Bank interest and charges paid
Credit transfers	Direct debits and standing orders paid
	Cheque drawn for cash
Closing balance c/d – bank overdraft	Closing balance c/d – cash in bank

AQA Examiner's tip

Don't forget, when a cheque is drawn for cash it will appear on both sides of the cash book. Debit the cash column and credit the bank column.

Activity

Cash book entries

State the entries that would appear in the cash book for the following transactions:

1. On 2 October paid a cheque for £135 to H Ahmed after taking £15 discount.

2. On 3 October withdrew cash from the bank of £50.

3. On 4 October received a cheque for £405 from R Wilkins having allowed discount of £45.

Balancing and closing off the cash book

At the end of the period, the **cash book** should be balanced and closed off.

1 Total all three debit column and all three credit columns.

2 To balance the cash column, enter the balancing figure in the side with the smaller total and label this 'Balance c/d' and date the final day of the accounting period. This balance is then transferred to the opposite side of the cash book as the opening balance. This should be labelled 'Balance b/d' and dated the first day of the next accounting period – see illustration below.

3 The totals of the discount allowed column and the discount received column are the final totals. These will eventually be posted to the general ledger to complete the double entry.

4 Exactly the same process should be carried out on the bank column to ascertain the bank balance.

Key terms

Cash book: book of original entry recording cash and cheque payments and receipts. The cash book also has columns to record discount received and discount allowed.

Illustration

How to balance and close off the cash book

Dr Date	Details	Discount allowed	Cash	Bank	Cash Book Date	Details	Discount received	Cash	Cr Bank
1 May	Green	48		988	2 May	Smith	22		276
3 May	Brown		84		3 May	Wages		116	
3 May	Bank		200		3 May	Jones			307
5 May	Black	26		342	3 May	Cash			200
					5 May	Abdul	8		106
					5 May	Balance c/d		168	441
		74	284	1,330			30	284	1,330
6 May	Balance b/d		168	441					

As you will see, the discount allowed column and discount received column are totalled, but the balance is NOT carried down. These totals are posted directly to the general ledger as follows:

Dr	Discount allowed account				Cr
Date	Details	£	Date	Details	£
6 May	Cash book	74			

Dr	Discount received account				Cr
Date	Details	£	Date	Details	£
			6 May	Cash book	30

Figure 2.12 *Discount allowed and received*

Note

It is important to recognise the difference between **cash discount** and **trade discount**.

Cash discount

Cash discount is a reduction in the amount owing to a supplier in return for settling their bills early. For example, a customer may be offered

Background knowledge

The difference between cash discount and trade discount is important because they are treated differently for invoicing and also in the preparation of accounts.

Key terms

Cash discount: a reduction in the amount owing to a supplier in return for settling their bills early (for example payment within 14 days).

Trade discount: offered to businesses in a similar line of business, as distinct from the general public, often as an incentive for buying in bulk quantities.

Discount received: discount we receive from suppliers for settling our bills promptly.

Discount allowed: discount we give to customers who settle their bills promptly.

Case study

Potter's Plants

Leon Potter set up his successful gardening business in 1989. He started selling small potting plants from his small garden and due to demand moved his business to larger premises in 1992, where he expanded and started to sell gardening equipment. He now employs 2 other full-time employees and 7 part-time employees.

2% discount if the bill is settled within 14 days. The customer has the choice of taking the discount if settled within the specified terms, or alternatively settling outside the terms and paying the full amount.

Cash discount is recorded separately in the cash book when the payment or receipt is processed.

Discount received is the discount taken when the business pays its supplier early.

Discount allowed is the discount allowed to a customer for early settlement of a sales invoice.

Trade discount

Trade discount is offered to businesses in a similar line of business, as distinct from the general public, often as an incentive for buying in bulk quantities.

Trade discount is NOT recorded separately in the books of account; it is simply a reduction of the net price of the goods or services supplied.

Activity

Sales day book

Enter the following invoices into the sales day book of Thompson Traders:

Invoice 2755	Tate Appliances	£345	No discount offered
Invoice 2756	H Parry	£1,460	Trade discount of 15%
Invoice 2757	D Lane & Co	£720	Cash discount of 5%

Illustration

How to record information in a cash book and balance it

Leon Potter maintains a manual set of books and the following transactions took place during the week ending 9 April.

4 April	Balances brought forward – cash in hand £53, bank overdraft £13,582.
4 April	Cash sales £312
5 April	Cheque paid to G Spooner £440 (discount taken £18)
5 April	Bank interest paid £128
6 April	Cheque received from Baird Ltd £89
8 April	Cheque drawn for use in making cash payments £900
8 April	Paid wages by cash £617
9 April	Cheque received from Lord & Co £5,238 (discount allowed £214)
9 April	Cash paid into the bank £312

Required

Record this information in a three-column cash book and balance the cash book at 10 April.

Explanations

Date	Transaction	Explanation
4 April	Balances brought forward – cash in hand £53, bank overdraft £13,582	The balance of cash brought forward is in hand and therefore an asset and a debit balance. The bank is overdrawn and therefore a liability and a credit balance.
4 April	Cash sales £312	Cash received will increase the asset of cash – debit cash.
5 April	Cheque paid to G Spooner £440 (discount taken £18)	Cheque paid will increase the overdraft, therefore credit bank. The discount of £18 is analysed into the discount received column.
5 April	Bank interest paid £128	Bank interest paid will increase the bank overdraft – credit bank.
6 April	Cheque received from Baird Ltd £89	The cheque received will reduce the overdraft – debit bank.
8 April	Cheque drawn for making cash payments £900	The cheque drawn for cash affects both the cash column and the bank column. The asset of cash is increased – debit cash. The liability of bank overdraft is also increased – credit bank.
8 April	Paid wages by cash £617	The wages paid will reduce the cash balance – credit cash.
9 April	Cheque received from Lord & Co £5,238 (discount allowed £214)	Cheque received will reduce the bank overdraft – debit bank. The discount of £214 will be analysed into the discount allowed column.
9 April	Cash paid into the bank £312	Cash banked will reduce the bank overdraft – debit bank. It will also reduce the balance of cash in hand – credit cash.

Solution

Dr					Cash Book				Cr
Date	Details	Discount allowed	Cash	Bank	Date	Details	Discount received	Cash	Bank
4 Apr	Balance b/d		53		4 Apr	Balance b/d			13,582
4 Apr	Cash sales		312		5 Apr	G Spooner	18		440
6 Apr	Baird Ltd			89	5 Apr	Bank Interest			128
8 Apr	Bank		900		8 Apr	Cash			900
9 Apr	Lord & Co	214		5,238	8 Apr	Wages		617	
9 Apr	Cash			312	9 Apr	Bank		312	
9 Apr	Balance c/d			9,411	9 Apr	Balance c/d		336	
		214	1,265	15,050			18	1,265	15,050
10 Apr	Balance b/d		336		10 Apr	Balance b/d			9,411

Key terms

General journal: book of original entry recording non-routine transactions that do not appear in the other books of original entry.

Background knowledge

Remember, the journal is not part of double entry bookkeeping – it is a subsidiary book listing transactions before they are entered into the accounts.

The general journal

The **general journal** is a book of original entry – a subsidiary book. The journal is used to record non-routine transactions or entries when no other book of original entry is suitable.

The journal will be used for:

- The correction of errors.
- Transferring amounts from one general ledger account to another.
- Processing the entry for depreciation.
- The purchase or sale of non-current assets.

Why is the journal necessary?

- It reduces the risk of fraud. The journal forms an integral part of the audit trail and as such reduces the possibility of unauthorised transactions being entered in the accounting records.
- It reduces the risk of incorrect entries by detailing the transactions as they are to be entered in the accounting records.
- It provides a permanent record of non-routine transactions entered in the accounting records.

The format of the journal

The journal is set out as follows:

Date	Details	Dr (£)	Cr (£)
30 June	Motor vehicle cost	4,500	
	Motor expenses		4,500
	Correction of posting error		

Figure 2.13 *Journal*

Note that it is good practice to provide a short narrative giving details of what the entry relates to.

Activity

General journal

Show the journal entries necessary to correct the following two errors

1 £110 cash received for sales has been incorrectly posted to the credit of purchases.

2 £415 paid for rent has been incorrectly posted to repairs.

Case study

Trent Gallery

On 1 October 2011, Brian Trent started his own business. He is an artist in his spare time and decided to open a small art gallery selling his own paintings and those of other local artists. Brian has an electronic cash register, but maintains a manual set of accounting records.

During the first week of trading, the following transactions took place and he was able to identify the source documents and the subsidiary books that had to be used to record them.

Transaction	Source document	Subsidiary book
Introduced capital of £20,000 into the bank account	Bank paying-in slip counterfoil	Cash book
Withdrew £500 cash from the bank	Cheque counterfoil	Cash book
Bought £1,300 paintings for resale on credit from Tony Jones	Purchase invoice	Purchases day book
Cash sales of £65	Till roll	Cash book
Bought goods for resale £368 from Gold Ltd	Purchase invoice	Purchases day book
Paid £120 into the bank	Bank paying-in slip counterfoil	Cash book
Sold goods to Ellison for £800 on credit	Sales invoice	Sales day book
Received a credit note for damaged goods returned to Gold Ltd £33	Purchase credit note	Purchases day book
Received a cheque for £800 from Ellison and paid this into the bank	Bank paying-in slip counterfoil	Cash book

Learning outcomes

As a result of studying this topic, you should now be able to:

- explain the purpose of the day books
- explain the process of posting entries from the day books into the ledgers
- explain the purpose and structure of the cash book
- explain the difference between cash discount and trade discount
- explain the purpose of the general journal

AQA Examination Style Questions

1 Complete the following table identifying the source document and subsidiary book for each transaction.

Transaction	Source document	Subsidiary Book
Purchased goods on credit from a supplier		
Paid for general expenses in cash		
Sold goods on credit to a customer		
Returned goods to a supplier which had been purchased on credit		
Customer paid amount due by credit transfer		
Purchased new fittings for shop on credit		

2   Anita owns Mercian Interior Designs. Her business's cash book for September 2011 is almost complete. On 28 September the following information is available.

Balance of cash in hand	£472
Balance of cash at bank (overdrawn)	£989
Total of discounts allowed column	£84
Total of discounts received column	£62

Transactions for the period 28–30 September 2011 were as follows:

Sept	28	Received cheque for £1,840 from customer, T Morris, in full settlement of amount due £1,895
	28	Paying-in slip counterfoil showed cash £380 paid into the bank account
	29	Paid Oregon Textiles Ltd a cheque for £1,330 in full settlement of the amount due having deducted a cash discount of 5%
	30	Received bank statement which showed the deduction of £118 for bank charges
	30	Bank notified Anita that a cheque from a customer, H Redford, £464 paid into the bank on 3 September had been dishonoured

Complete the cash book for September 2011. Balance the cash and bank columns. Total the discount columns and post the totals to the general ledger.

3   Jamie Anderson is responsible for recording transactions in the subsidiary books of the business by which he is employed. During July 2011 the business's transactions included the following.

July	7	An invoice was received from payable, Carolus Ltd, for some new office equipment £3,220
	11	The owner of the business withdrew inventory for personal use, value £290
	16	Jamie was asked to correct an error in the accounts. The account of a trade receivable, Ace Products Ltd, has been debited with sales of £800. The sale had, in fact, been made to Ace Supplies.
	30	A credit note was received from Carolus Ltd, showing a deduction of £280 in the amount due for the office equipment received on 7 July

Prepare the business's general journal for July 2011.

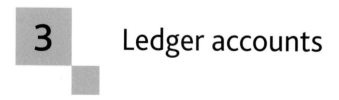

3   Ledger accounts

In this topic you will learn:

■ how to post transactions from subsidiary books into ledgers

■ how to balance and close off accounts.

Periodically, the subsidiary books will be totalled and the totals will be transferred into the ledger system.

Ledgers are an essential part of the double entry bookkeeping system, containing all of the information grouped together for a specific customer, supplier or general ledger account.

Sales ledger

The **sales ledger** contains personal accounts for each individual customer to whom we sell goods or provide services on a credit basis as distinct from a cash sale basis. The account summarises all transactions with a particular customer and shows what they owe the business. A typical sales ledger account will contain some or all of the items detailed below.

Dr	Green & Co					Cr
Date	**Details**	**£**	**Date**	**Details**		**£**
1 Nov	Balance b/d	5,425	30 Nov	Bank		9,780
30 Nov	Sales day book	11,653	30 Nov	Discounts allowed		236
30 Nov	**Returned cheques**	112	30 Nov	Sales returns day book		270
			30 Nov	**Contras**		340
			30 Nov	**Bad debts written off**		50
			30 Nov	Balance c/d		6,514
		17,190				17,190
1 June	Balance b/d	6,514				

Figure 2.14 *Sales ledger*

Note that the account commences with the balance brought down at the start of the period as a debit balance since customers who owe the business money are receivables.

As you will see later, the sales ledger control account mirrors each individual personal account, but is a total account including *all* transactions that are posted to *all* of the customer accounts.

Purchases ledger

The **purchases ledger** (see Figure 2.15) contains personal accounts for each individual supplier from whom we purchase goods or services on a credit basis as distinct from a cash sale basis. The account summarises all transactions with a particular supplier and shows what the business owes to them. A typical purchases ledger account will contain some or all of the items detailed below.

Dr	Brown & Co				Cr
Date	**Details**	**£**	**Date**	**Details**	**£**
30 Nov	Bank	6,411	1 Nov	Balance b/d	3,440
30 Nov	Discounts received	58	30 Nov	Purchases day book	5,285
30 Nov	Purchases returns day book	108	30 Nov	Cancelled cheques	312
30 Nov	Contras	213			
30 Nov	Balance c/d	2,247			
		9,037			9,037
			1 Dec	Balance b/d	2,247

Figure 2.15 *Purchases ledger*

Note that the account commences with the balance brought down at the start of the period as a credit balance since suppliers to whom the business money owes are payables.

As you will see later, the purchase ledger control account mirrors each individual personal account, but is a total account including *all* transactions that are posted to *all* of the supplier accounts.

Balancing and closing off personal ledger accounts

Periodically, all ledger accounts are balanced and closed off. This process involves totalling both sides of the account and entering the balancing figure in the side with the smaller total to enable the account to balance. This balancing figure is then carried down on the opposite side as the commencing figure for the next accounting period.

Example 1 – debit and credit column totals are the same

In this example, since both totals are identical, the account is totalled and ruled off.

Dr			A Smith		Cr
Date	Details	£	Date	Details	£
1 Nov	Balance b/d	3,200	30 Nov	Bank	7,360
30 Nov	Sales day book	4,160			
		7,360			7,360

Figure 2.16 *Example 1*

Example 2 – debit and credit column totals are not equal

In this example, the totals of the debit and credit columns are not equal, so the difference between the two columns (£9,630) is entered on the credit side to balance the account and is carried down on the debit side as the opening balance for the next accounting period.

Dr			A Jones		Cr
Date	Details	£	Date	Details	£
1 Nov	Balance b/d	2,480	30 Nov	Bank	4,500
30 Nov	Sales day book	11,650	30 Nov	Balance c/d	9,630
		14,130			14,130
1 Dec	Balance b/d	9,630			

Figure 2.17 *Example 2*

Activity

Balancing sales ledger account

Balance the following sales ledger account for Williams & Co

Dr			Williams & Co		Cr
Date	Details	£	Date	Details	£
1 Feb	Balance b/d	17,536	28 Feb	Sales returns day book	512
28 Feb	Sales day book	62,508	28 Feb	Bank	61,227
			28 Feb	Discount allowed	533
			28 Feb	Contra	300

General ledger

The **general ledger** contains all of the remaining impersonal accounts. Impersonal accounts are those accounts that do not relate to a person or another business and these are either

- **real accounts**, which record non-current assets, for example machinery or motor vehicles, or
- **nominal accounts**, which record revenue and expense items, for example sales, purchases, stationery, etc.
- The balances from the general ledger form the basis of the trial balance.

Balancing and closing off general ledger accounts

The process of **balancing off** and closing off general ledger accounts depends on the nature of the section of the income statement.

Example 1 – income statement (trading section)

An income statement item such as sales, purchases, carriage inwards, etc. will be closed off by transfer to the trading section of the income statement.

Dr			Sales			Cr
Date	Details	£	Date	Details		£
30 Nov	*Income statement*	*88,949*	30 Nov	Sales day book		86,467
			30 Nov	Bank		2,482
		88,949				88,949

Figure 2.18 *Income statement*

Example 2 – income statement (profit and loss section)

A section of the income statement item such as discount allowed, stationery, etc. will be closed off by transfer to the profit and loss section of the income statement.

Dr			Stationery			Cr
Date	Details	£	Date	Details		£
30 Nov	Purchases day book	2,144	*30 Nov*	*Income statement*		*2,282*
30 Nov	Bank	138				
		2,282				2,282

Figure 2.19 *Income statement*

Example 3 – statement of financial position (balance sheet)

A statement of financial position (balance sheet) item such as machinery or cash at bank will be closed off by carrying the balance down to the start of the next accounting period.

Dr				Machinery			Cr
Date	Details		£	Date	Details		£
1 Nov	Balance b/d		18,450	*30 Nov*	*Balance c/d*		*19,810*
30 Nov	Journal		1,360				
			19,810				19,810
1 Dec	*Balance b/d*		*19,810*				

Figure 2.20 *Statement of financial position (balance sheet)*

Illustration

How to balance and close off ledger accounts

The following transactions took place at Khan Kitchens during the first week of May.

All sales and purchases are made on credit.

1 May   Purchased goods from Byfield Ltd for £430.
3 May   Purchased goods from Lee Units for £2,795.
3 May   Sold goods to Garside Kitchens for £978.
3 May   Purchased goods from BM Modules £3,570.
4 May   Received a credit note from Lee Units for £322.
4 May   Sold goods to H Brunning for £1,880.
5 May   Sold goods to Malcolm & Co for £3,094.
5 May   Sent a credit note to Garside Kitchens for £85.
5 May   Purchased goods from Byfield Ltd for £5,337.
6 May   Sold goods to Garside Kitchens for £2,680.

Required

Enter the above transactions in the appropriate day books of Khan Kitchens, complete the postings to the purchase ledger, sales ledger and general ledger, and balance and close off all accounts at 7 May.

Approach

- Ascertain which day books are to be used for each transaction.
- Post the transactions into the relevant day books.
- Total the day books.
- Post the individual items from the day books into the personal accounts in the sales ledger and purchases ledger.
- Post the totals from the day books into the general ledger.
- Balance and close off all ledger accounts.

Solution

Sales day book		
Date	Customer	Amount (£)
3 May	Garside Kitchens	978
4 May	H Brunning	1,880
5 May	Malcolm & Co	3,094
6 May	Garside Kitchens	2,680
		8,632

Purchases day book

Date	Supplier	Amount (£)
1 May	Byfield Ltd	430
3 May	Lee Units	2,795
3 May	BM Modules	3,570
5 May	Byfield Ltd	5,337
		12,132

Sales returns day book

Date	Customer	Amount (£)
5 May	Garside Kitchens	85
		85

Purchases returns day book

Date	Supplier	Amount (£)
4 May	Lee Units	322
		322

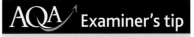

AQA Examiner's tip

If you are asked to balance an account, don't forget to bring down the balance.

Sales ledger

Dr				Garside Kitchens	Cr
Date	Details	£	Date	Details	£
3 May	Sales day book	978	5 May	Sales returns day book	85
6 May	Sales day book	2,680	7 May	Balance c/d	3,573
		3,658			3,658
8 May	Balance b/d	3,573			

Dr				H Brunning	Cr
Date	Details	£	Date	Details	£
4 May	Sales day book	1,880	7 May	Balance c/d	1,880
		1,880			1,880
8 May	Balance b/d	1,880			

Dr				Malcolm & Co	Cr
Date	Details	£	Date	Details	£
5 May	Sales day book	3,094	7 May	Balance c/d	3,094
		3,094			3,094
8 May	Balance b/d	3,094			

Purchases ledger

Dr	Byfield Ltd				Cr
Date	Details	£	Date	Details	£
7 May	Balance c/d	5,767	1 May	Purchases day book	430
			5 May	Purchases day book	5,337
		5,767			5,767
			8 May	Balance b/d	5,767

Dr	Lee Units				Cr
Date	Details	£	Date	Details	£
4 May	Purchases returns day book	322	3 May	Purchases day book	2,795
7 May	Balance c/d	2,473			
		2,795			2,795
			8 May	Balance b/d	2,473

Dr	BM Modules				Cr
Date	Details	£	Date	Details	£
7 May	Balance c/d	3,570	3 May	Purchases day book	3,570
		3,570			3,570
			8 May	Balance b/d	3,570

General ledger

Dr	Sales				Cr
Date	Details	£	Date	Details	£
7 May	Income statement	8,632	7 May	Sales day book	8,632
		8,632			8,632

Dr	Sales returns				Cr
Date	Details	£	Date	Details	£
7 May	Sales returns day book	85	7 May	Income statement	85
		85			85

Dr	Purchases				Cr
Date	Details	£	Date	Details	£
7 May	Purchases day book	12,132	7 May	Income statement	12,132
		12,132			12,132

Dr	Purchases returns				Cr
Date	Details	£	Date	Details	£
7 May	Income statement	322	3 May	Purchases returns day book	322
		322			322

AQA✓ **Examiner's tip**

- Note that all of the balances c/d are dated 7 May, the last day of the accounting period, whereas all of the balances b/d are dated 8 May, the first day of the next accounting period.

- The four general ledger accounts are closed on 7 May. The closing entry shows the transfer of the account balance to the income statement.

Link

For more information on ledger accounts, see Chapter 7, page 90.

Learning outcomes

As a result of studying this topic, you should now be able to:

- post transactions from the subsidiary books to the sales ledger and purchases ledger
- balance and close off personal accounts in the sales ledger and purchases ledger
- balance and close off general ledger accounts

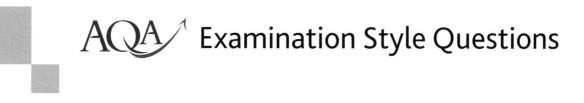

AQA Examination Style Questions

1   Dellon Systems is a business which provides specialist computer software. The following personal accounts appeared in the business's books on 1 October 2011.

Ledger	Account	Balance 1 October (£)
Purchases ledger	Parfield Ltd	1,900 (Cr)
Sales ledger	Hammond Bros	2,440 (Dr)
	Intratex Ltd	1,720 (Dr)
	JPL Ltd	640 (Dr)

The following extracts have been taken from the subsidiary books of Dellon Systems.

Purchases day book

			£
Oct	22	Parfield Ltd	3,321
	29	Parfield Ltd	1,435
			4,756

Returns inwards day book

			£
Oct	16	Hammond Bros	442

Returns outwards day book

			£
Oct	26	Parfield Ltd	174

Sales day book

			£
Oct	4	Hammond Bros	1,312
	11	Intratex Ltd	2,070
	18	Hammond Bros	984
			4,366

Dr	Cash Book (Extracts)							Cr		
			Discounts					Discounts		
			Allowed	Bank				Received	Bank	
			£	£				£	£	
Oct	3	Intratex Ltd		1,720	Oct	14	Parfield Ltd	95	1,805	
	27	Hammond Bros	61	2,379		16	Intratex Ltd			
							(returned cheque)		1,720	

General Journal				£	£
Oct	30	Bad debts		640	
		JPL Ltd			640
		Trade receivable written off as a bad debt			

Record this information in the purchases ledger and sales ledger. Balance the accounts on 31 October 2011.

3 Verification of accounting records

In the previous chapter, you have learned how to account for a range of transactions from source document, through subsidiary books into the ledger system. This chapter builds on that knowledge by looking at various aspects of verification of the accounting records.

Having processed transactions into the accounting records, we now need to verify the accuracy of the records and the following techniques enable this to be done

- Trial balance to check the arithmetical accuracy of the ledger accounts.
- Sales and purchases ledger control accounts to check the arithmetical accuracy of the sales and purchases ledgers.
- Bank reconciliation statements to check the arithmetical accuracy of the cash book when compared to the bank statement.
- It is important to recognise that these techniques are checking the arithmetical accuracy – they do not of course guarantee that everything has been posted into the correct account.
- As a result, we shall look at different types of errors, how to correct errors that are revealed and what effect those errors may have on both the trial balance and the income statement.
- It is important to not only be able to prepare trial balances, control accounts and bank reconciliation statements, but you must also be aware of the benefits and limitations of these techniques and be prepared to answer written questions on this subject area.

1 Trial balance

In this topic you will learn:

- to understand the role, presentation and limitations of the trial balance
- how to identify and correct different types of errors affecting the trial balance and the effect that errors may have on the calculation of profit.

The trial balance is simply a listing of all the account ledger balances on a given date. As we have already seen, for every debit there must be equal and corresponding credits. Providing the double entry has been accurately carried out, the total of all debits will equal the total of all credits and the trial balance will balance.

Presentation of the trial balance

A trial balance will be presented as follows

ABC		
Trial balance at 30 June 2011		
Account	Dr (£)	Cr (£)

Figure 3.1 *A trial balance*

Background knowledge

The trial balance is the intermediate step in the preparation of the final accounts of a business. It gathers together all of the balances from the ledgers and proves the arithmetical accuracy of them.

AQA Examiner's tip

- A trial balance should always have a heading as shown in Figure 3.1.

- You will often be presented with just a list of balances and asked to produce a trial balance. Remember the rules of double entry stated earlier.

- When deciding which account to debit and which account to credit, you may find it helpful to recall the mnemonic '**DEAD CLIC**'.

Activity

Trial balance

Explain why a trial balance should always balance.

Key terms

Bank overdraft: a form of loan where the bank allows a customer to be overdrawn (make total payments in excess of total receipts) up to a specified limit.

Mortgage: a long term loan, usually secured against assets.

Illustration

How to prepare a trial balance

Chris's bookkeeper has extracted the following list of balances at the financial year end, 31 October 2011 and has asked for a trial balance to be prepared at that date.

	£
Bank overdraft	5,150
Capital account at 1 November 2010	56,900
Carriage inwards	1,750
Carriage outwards	840
Cash and cash equivalents	110
Drawings	24,000
Fixtures and fittings at cost	34,200
Inventory at 1 November 2010	54,080
Mortgage on premises (repayable 2017)	50,000
Motor running expenses	3,370
Motor vehicle at cost	4,200
Premises at cost	85,000
Purchases	92,150
Rent and rates	5,200
Returns inwards	960
Returns outwards	390
Sales	206,370
Stationery and advertising	1,860
Trade payables	5,320
Trade receivables	4,210
Wages	12,200

Approach

Work down the list of balances and decide whether they are a debit entry or a credit entry.

Solution

Trial balance at 31 October 2011

	Dr (£)	Cr (£)
Bank overdraft		5,150
Capital account at 1 November 2010		56,900
Carriage inwards	1,750	
Carriage outwards	840	
Cash in hand	110	
Drawings	24,000	
Fixtures and fittings at cost	34,200	
Inventory at 1 November 2010	54,080	
Mortgage on premises (repayable 2017)		50,000
Motor running expenses	3,370	
Motor vehicle at cost	4,200	
Premises at cost	85,000	
Purchases	92,150	
Rent and rates	5,200	
Returns inwards	960	
Returns outwards		390
Sales		206,370
Stationery and advertising	1,860	

Trade payables		5,320
Trade receivables	4,210	
Wages	12,200	
	324,130	324,130

Trial balance errors

Although the trial balance shown in the illustration above does balance, it does not necessarily mean that everything has been posted into the correct account or that all of the transactions have been recorded correctly or indeed have been recorded at all.

Some errors will affect the trial balance whilst some will not affect the balancing of the trial balance.

Errors that will NOT be revealed by the trial balance

- **Errors of omission.** Where both sides of the transaction, debit and credit, have been omitted from the records.
- **Compensating error.** Where errors on the debit side equal errors on the credit side and they cancel each other out.
- **Error of commission.** Where an amount is posted to an incorrect account of the correct type. For example Andrew Smith account instead of Alf Smith account.
- **Error of principle.** Where an amount is posted to an incorrect class of account. For example, motor repairs (an expense) are posted to motor vehicles (an asset).
- **Error of original entry.** Where an error is made transferring an amount from the source document into the book of original entry. As a result the double entry for the result will be for the wrong amount.
- **Error of reversal.** Where the account that should have been debited has been credited and the amount that should have been credited has been debited.

Errors that WILL be revealed by the trial balance

- **Transposition errors.** Where, for example, one entry has been posted as £54 and another incorrectly transposed and posted as £45.
- **Addition errors.** In the trial balance itself or in a general ledger account.
- **Posting errors.** Where one side of the transaction is posted to the wrong side of an account.
- **Partial omission error.** Where one side of the transaction is not posted.
- **Unequal posting error.** Where the debit side of the posting does not equal the credit side.

If the trial balance does not balance

Extracting a trial balance immediately verifies the arithmetical accuracy of the ledger. If the trial balance does not balance, until such time as the errors are identified and corrected, the difference may be entered into a **suspense account** to temporarily enable the trial balance totals to agree.

Errors and suspense accounts

When the reason for errors is discovered, a journal entry should be processed to remove the amount(s) from the suspense account by transfer into the correct account.

Examiner's tip

- Remember the mnemonic DEAD CLIC to help you.
- Debits – Expenditure, Assets, Drawings
- Credits – Liabilities, Income, Capital

Activity

Trial balance errors

James has discovered an error in his accounting records. A payment of £7,000 for machinery has been debited to purchases account.

1 Identify the name of this type of error.

2 Explain why the trial balance should still balance.

Background knowledge

It is very important to recognise different types of error. As you will see in this section, some errors do affect the balancing of the trial balance, others do not.

Key terms

Suspense account: a temporary account used to post a difference in the trial balance (i.e. the total of the debit side does not equal the total of the credit side) until such time as the differences are identified.

Illustration

How to deal with suspense accounts

The trial balance of Michie & Co. contains errors and a suspense account has been opened with a balance of £90 Dr. It is discovered that the difference was caused by a posting error. A cheque for £540 had been posted to motor expenses account as £450.

To correct the error, £90 (£540 – £450) must be removed from suspense account and transferred to motor expenses account, which is where it should have been posted.

The journal entry to correct this will therefore be

Debit	Motor expenses	£90
Credit	Suspense account	£90

Correction of transposition error

As a result of this transfer, the suspense account now has a zero balance and is no longer required and motor expenses account now reflects the correct figure.

Case study

Fancy Goods Enterprises

Fancy Goods Enterprises was set up in 2002 by two sisters, Karen Learmonth and Rachel Hamalienko. They sell gifts and souvenirs and they currently have two shops and are well known in the local area.

Illustration

How to make entries in the suspense account and show the opening balance

Fancy Goods Enterprises is a successful business, but the inexperienced bookkeeper has made a number of errors throughout the year. The trial balance was drawn up as at 31 March 2011 but the totals did not agree and the following errors have been discovered.

1. The purchases account has been overcast by £4,500.
2. The receivables' total includes £650 that has been written off as a bad debt.
3. Discount received of £300 has been entered on the debit of the account.
4. A cheque for £673, payable to Sunshine Products Ltd has been entered in the account of Sunmaster Products in error.
5. The credit balance in the rent payable account has been brought down as £990; it should have been £909.

Required

You have been asked to make any necessary entries in the suspense account to correct these errors, and show the opening balance.

Dr		Suspense account		Cr
Details	£	Details		£

Approach

You are not given the opening balance on the suspense account, so take each of the errors in turn, assessing the effect each will have on the suspense account. Complete the suspense account with all relevant amounts and enter the difference as the opening balance.

1 Purchases must be reduced by £4,500 – credit purchases, debit suspense account.

2 Receivables must be reduced by £650 – credit receivables, debit suspense account.

3 Discount received of £300 has been entered on the debit of the account, whereas it should have been entered to the credit of the account. As a result, the correction has to be for £600 – £300 to cancel the debit entry and another £300 to place the entry on the credit side of discounts received account. Debit suspense account and credit discounts received account with £600.

4 This error must be corrected through the purchases ledger, but since the cheque has been processed through the correct ledger, but an incorrect personal account, this will not affect the suspense account. No entry is necessary.

5 Rent payable must be increased (debited) by £81 – debit rent payable and credit suspense account.

Solution

The completed suspense account will be as follows

Dr		Suspense account		Cr
Details	£	Details		£
Purchases	4,500	Opening balance		5,669
Receivables	650	Rent payable		81
Discount received	600			
	5,750			5,750

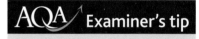

AQA Examiner's tip

Remember, only one side of the correcting entry should appear on the suspense account, the corresponding entry appears on the other account affected by the error.

What is the importance of the trial balance?

■ It checks the accuracy of the bookkeeping.

■ It is the stepping stone to the preparation of financial statements – the income statement and statement of financial position (balance sheet).

Assessing the effect of errors on profit

Errors will often affect the calculation of profit. This could apply to errors that do affect the trial balance or, indeed, errors that do not affect the trial balance.

Examination questions may concentrate on the effect that errors have on the calculation of profit and require the calculation of an amended profit.

AQA Examiner's tip

Bear in mind that errors affecting only statement of financial position (balance sheet) items will not affect profit.

Illustration

How to calculate the correct profit

A trainee accountant for Dublin & Co. produced a draft income statement that showed a profit for the year ended 31 March 2011 of £17,690. Her supervisor subsequently discovered the following errors.

1   The purchases day book had been undercast by £520.

2   The cost of repairs to a delivery van of £450 had been debited to the motor vehicles account.

3   A payment of £500 for insurance had been completely omitted from the accounts.

4   A cheque for £2,300 received from B Harrison, a receivable, had been credited to the account of B Harris.

5   Discount received of £1,300 had been charged as an expense in the income statement.

6   The closing inventory had been recorded in the income statement as £3,000. The correct figure was £300.

Required

You are required to calculate the correct net profit. It is important to show clearly whether each adjustment is added, subtracted or has no effect on the profit calculation.

Corrected profit for the year ended 31 March 2011

	£
Profit as given	17,690
1	
2	
3	
4	
5	
6	
Corrected profit	

Approach

Take each point in turn and decide firstly whether it has any effect on the profit calculation and secondly what that effect is.

1   The purchases day book had been undercast by £520, so as a result purchases have been understated by the same amount. Increasing purchases will reduce the profit.

2   The cost of repairs to a delivery van of £450 had been debited to the motor vehicles account. Since motor vehicles are a non-current asset, correcting this error of principle will increase the expenses of delivery van repair and therefore reduce the profit.

3   Correcting the omission of the payment of £500 for insurance will increase expenses and therefore reduce the profit.

4   This error of commission must be corrected through the sales ledger, but since the receipt has been processed through the correct ledger, but an incorrect personal account, this will not affect the profit.

5   Discount received of £1,300 had been charged as an expense in the income statement, but it should be shown as income. Correcting this error will increase the profit by £2,600. Firstly, £1,300 to cancel the expense and secondly a further £1,300 to process the income.

6   Closing inventory has been overstated by £2,700. Since closing inventory is subtracted from the cost of sales, £2,700 too much has been taken away. Correcting this error will increase the cost of sales by £2,700 and therefore reduce the profit.

Solution

Corrected profit for the year ended 31 March 2011

			£
	Profit as given		17,690
1	Purchases undercast	Subtract	520
2	Delivery van repairs	Subtract	450
3	Insurance omitted	Subtract	500
4	Error of commission	No effect	
5	Discount received	Add	2,600
6	Closing inventory overstated	Subtract	2,700
	Corrected profit		**16,120**

Learning outcomes

As a result of studying this topic, you should now be able to:

- state the purpose and importance of the trial balance

- identify errors that both affect and do not affect the trial balance

- correct errors by the use of the suspense account

- assess the effect that errors will have on the calculation of profit

AQA Examination Style Questions

1 Colin Patterson is the owner of a retail business. On 31 December 2011, his business trial balance was as shown below, with the following balances still to be recorded.

	£
Bank overdraft	3,650
Carriage inwards	1,234
Carriage outwards	837
Discounts allowed	437
Discounts received	229
Returns inwards	1,449
Returns outwards	887
Trade payables	7,497
Trade receivables	11,372

	Dr	Cr
	£	£
Bank overdraft		
Capital		84,500
Carriage inwards		

Carriage outwards		
Discounts allowed		
Discounts received		
Drawings	27,590	
Inventory at 1 January 2011	11,400	
Non-current assets	73,500	
Operating expenses	44,278	
Purchases	137,582	
Returns inwards		
Returns outwards		
Sales		212,916
Trade payables		
Trade receivables		

(a) Complete the trial balance at 31 December 2011.

Colin has found the task of preparing the trial balance very time consuming and has said he does not really see the point of producing a list of information which is already available in the ledger accounts.

(b) Do you agree with Colin? Give reasons for your answer and assess the technique of producing trial balances.

2   During a recent financial period the following errors were made in the accounts of a business. None of the errors affected the agreement of the trial balance totals.

	Error	Type of error
1	An invoice received from a supplier for £654 was recorded in the purchases day book as being for £564	
2	A returns inwards for £117 from a trade receivable, S Macintyre, was credited to the account of S MacArthur.	
3	Cash sales of £940 were recorded in the accounts as Dr Cash £940 Cr Sales £900; the total of the discounts allowed column in the cash book was mis-totalled at £40 rather the correct figure of £80.	
4	A cheque counterfoil for business rates £620 was entirely overlooked	
5	The purchase of some new office equipment £2,300 was debited to the purchases account.	
6	The entries made for the payment of a trade payable, L Mendez, by cheque £630 were: Dr Bank £630, Cr L Mendez £630	

(a) Identify the type of error made in each case 1–6 above.
(b) Prepare journal entries to correct the errors.

3 An accounts clerk was unable to get the totals of a trial balance to agree. The totals were as follows:

	Dr	Cr
	£	£
	172,300	170,900

The accounts clerk found the following errors in the ledger accounts which had caused the disagreement in the trial balance totals.

(i) cash sales of £23,670 had been correctly entered in the cash book, but had been credited to the sales account as £23,170.

(ii) the total of the returns in day book, £300, had not been posted to the ledger account.

(iii) interest received of £1,200 had been correctly entered in the cash book, but had not been posted to the interest received account.

(a) Prepare journal entries to correct these errors.

(b) Prepare the suspense account.

4 When Tiffany Cheung prepared her business's trial balance on 31 October 2011 the totals failed to agree. Tiffany checked the accounting records and discovered the following errors.

(i) The receipt of £660 from a trade receivable, N Somaya, had been correctly entered in the cash book but had not been posted to the trade receivable account.

(ii) The total of the returns outwards day book, £683, had not been posted to the general ledger

(iii) Discounts allowed of £240 had been credited to the account of Alice Hardy instead of Alison Harwick.

(iv) A cheque for £790 in payment of rent had been entered in the accounts as £970.

(v) The total of the discounts received column in the cash book, £330, had been posted to the debit side of the discounts allowed account.

(vi) A payment of a trade payable, Suparex Ltd, £1,040, had been debited in the cash book and credited to the trade payable's account.

(a) Prepare journal entries to correct these errors.

(b) Prepare the suspense account and identify the original difference in the trial balance totals.

5 Derek Alton recently prepared the end of year income statement for his business. The income statement showed a draft profit of £38,300 for the year ended 30 November 2011. However, the following errors in the accounting records were discovered.

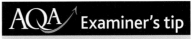

AQA Examiner's tip

When answering a question of this nature, avoid using plus and minus signs or brackets. Always use the terminology indicated in the question – in this case add or subtract. Similarly where you wish to indicate that there will be no change to the profit, be specific with your response, do not simply leave blank.

1 The purchases figure was understated by £720 in the income statement.

2 No entry was made for depreciation of equipment, £4,400, in the income statement.

3 Business rates due but unpaid, £680, was overlooked when preparing the income statement.

4 The bank loan account was incorrectly balanced. The balance brought down should have been £23,500, not £22,500.

5 The expense 'loan interest £990' was added to the gross profit rather than deducted.

6 Carriage inwards, £390, was recorded in the profit and loss section of the income statement.

7 Returns outwards £2,270 was overlooked when preparing the income statement.

Prepare a statement showing the effect of correcting these errors on the draft profit for the year ended 30 November 2011.

2   Bank reconciliation statement

Background knowledge

Businesses will prepare a bank reconciliation regularly. This enables the early detection of any errors in the cash book, but also acts as a deterrent to fraud.

AQA Examiner's tip

Remember, if the opening balance as per the cash book is overdrawn, unpresented cheques will be **deducted** and outstanding lodgements **added**.

Key terms

Unpresented cheques: cheques that have been drawn and entered in the cash book, but have not yet been presented to the bank for payment.

Outstanding (uncleared) lodgements: bank deposits that have been recorded in the cash book but have not yet been processed by the bank.

Direct debit: where authority is granted by the business to a third party for fixed or variable payments to be made at the request of that third party.

Standing order: where a fixed payment is made at regular intervals by the bank on the instructions of the business.

The purpose of the bank reconciliation statement is to reconcile the balance as per the cash book with the balance as per the bank statement.

In other words, *internal* records (the cash book) can be reconciled with *external* records (the bank statements).

The reasons why these two balances may not agree are:

- ■ **Unpresented cheques.** Cheques drawn but not yet presented for payment through the bank account.
- ■ **Outstanding lodgements.** Cash or cheques paid into the bank that have not yet been recorded on the bank statement.
- ■ Items that have been debited or credited directly to the bank account that have not yet been entered in the cash book (e.g. bank interest or charges, **direct debits**, **standing orders**, etc.).

Bank reconciliation statement – structure

The structure of a bank reconciliation statement is as follows:

Balance as per cash book		XXX
Add: unpresented cheques	XXX	
	XXX	
	XXX	XXX
		XXX
Less: outstanding lodgements	XXX	
	XXX	XXX
Balance as per bank statement		XXX

Figure 3.2 *Bank reconciliation statement*

The bank reconciliation may also be produced commencing with the balance as per the bank statement. In this case, unpresented cheques should be deducted (they will reduce the balance in the bank when they are presented) and outstanding lodgements should be added.

Preparing a bank reconciliation statement

Step 1   Tick all items that appear on the bank statement and also in the cash book.

Step 2   Enter into the cash book any items that appear on the bank statement, but not in the cash book.

Step 3   Balance the bank columns of the cash book and carry down the closing balance.

Step 4   Start the bank reconciliation statement by entering the closing balance as per the cash book.

Step 5   Unticked payments in the cash book are the unpresented cheques. Enter these into the bank reconciliation.

Step 6 Unticked receipts in the cash book are outstanding lodgements. Enter these into the bank reconciliation.

Step 7 Calculate the closing balance on the bank reconciliation statement. This should agree with the balance as per the bank statement.

Remember

- A **bank statement** is a record of the customer's account in the books of the bank. As a result, the entries are opposite to the entries in the customer's cash book.
- The debit column of a bank statement contains payments <u>out</u> of the bank. The credit column of a bank statement contains payments <u>into</u> the bank.
- A credit balance on the bank statement indicates cash in the bank. A debit balance on the bank statement indicates an overdrawn balance.

Illustration

How to update a cashbook and prepare a bank reconciliation

Ling Yeung has recently received her bank statement dated 17 March 2012 and asks you to prepare a bank reconciliation statement at that date.

The bank statement and an extract from her cash book are shown below:

Bank Statement for Ling Yeung dated 17 March 2012

Date	Details	Dr (£)	Cr (£)	Balance (£)
7 March	Balance brought forward			1,812 Cr
7 March	Cheque 488246	100		1,712 Cr
10 March	Credit		1,615	3,327 Cr
10 March	Direct debit – business rates	168		3,159 Cr
10 March	Credit		2,607	5,766 Cr
12 March	Cheque 488245	42		5,724 Cr
12 March	Cheque 488247	117		5,607 Cr
13 March	Standing order – JK Finance	210		5,397 Cr
13 March	Credit transfer – XY Clothing		446	5,843 Cr
13 March	Cheque 488249	635		5,208 Cr
17 March	Bank charges	26		5,182 Cr
17 March	Cheque 488251	963		4,219 Cr

Ling Yeung. Cash book extract

Dr						Cr
Date	Details	£	Date	Details		£
7 March	Balance b/d	1,812	7 March	488245 P Davies		42
7 March	B West & Co	1,615	7 March	488246 Cash		100
10 March	Ford Clothing	2,607	10 March	488247 S Keene		117

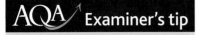

17 March	Wye Leisurewear	3,260	10 March	488248 Foley & Co	1,063
			10 March	488249 HK Clothing	635
			11 March	488250 Sawyer Ltd	390
			12 March	488251 D Alsop	963
			12 March	488252 Lee Motors	112

Required

Update the cash book at 17 March 2012 and prepare a bank reconciliation statement at that date.

Approach

1 Tick all amounts that appear on both the bank statement and in the cash book.
2 Enter all items that are unticked on the bank statement into the cash book.
3 Close off the cash book and carry down the balance.
4 Start the bank reconciliation statement by entering the closing balance from the updated cash book.
5 Add all unpresented cheques (unticked items from the credit side of the cash book).
6 Deduct all outstanding lodgements (unticked items from the debit side of the cash book).
7 The balance on the bank reconciliation statement should now agree with the balance in the cash book.

Solution

Ling Yeung – Updated cash book					
Dr					Cr
Date	Details	£	Date	Details	£
7 March	Balance b/d	1,812	7 March	488245 P Davies	42
7 March	B West & Co	1,615	7 March	488246 Cash	100
10 March	Ford Clothing	2,607	10 March	488247 S Keene	117
17 March	Wye Leisurewear	3,260	10 March	488248 Foley & Co	1,063
17 March	**Credit transfer XY Clothing**	**446**	10 March	488249 HK Clothing	635
			11 March	488250 Sawyer Ltd	390
			12 March	488251 D Alsop	963
			12 March	488252 Lee Motors	112
			17 March	**Direct debit business rates**	**168**
			17 March	**Standing order JK Finance**	**210**
			17 March	**Bank charges**	**26**
			17 March	Balance c/d	5,914
		9,740			9,740
18 March	Balance b/d	5,914			

Ling Yeung – Bank reconciliation statement at 17 March 2012			
		£	£
Balance per cash book			5,914
Add: Unpresented cheques	488248	1,063	
	488250	390	
	488252	112	1,565
			7,479
Deduct: Outstanding lodgements Wye Leisurewear			3,260
Balance per bank statement			4,219

What is the importance of the bank reconciliation statement?

▨ It enables any errors in the cash book to be corrected.

▨ It enables any errors on the bank statement to be investigated and notified to the bank for correction.

▨ It enables any missing entries in the cash book to be accounted for.

▨ It acts as a deterrent to fraud because the bank statement is an independent accounting record, prepared by the bank, providing the means to verify entries in the cash book.

▨ It enables any out-of-date cheques to be identified (over six months old) and cancelled in the cash book.

Learning outcomes

As a result of studying this topic, you should now be able to:

▨ state the purpose and importance of the bank reconciliation

▨ update the cash book by reference to the bank statement

▨ prepare a bank reconciliation statement

Activity

Explain the difference between a direct debit and a standing order.

AQA Examination Style Questions

1   On 4 December 2011, the following bank statement covering November was received by the head of the accounts team at Riverford Wholesale.

MIDSHIRE BANK plc					
Bank Statement for RIVERFORD WHOLESALE					
Date		Details	Dr	Cr	Balance
			£	£	£
Nov	1	Balance			4,155	Cr
	3	229203 KLK Ltd	2,325		1,830	Cr
	11	Sundry credit		4,782	6,612	Cr
	13	CHR	189		6,423	Cr

	18	229204	1,012		5,411	Cr
	21	DD National Telecoms plc	787		4,624	Cr
	23	Sundry credit		3,114	7,738	Cr
	25	Credit transfer: Leo Cole Ltd		883	8,621	Cr
	26	229206 Westby Traders	1,336		7,285	Cr
	27	SO Riverford Properties Ltd	665		6,620	Cr
	28	Dishonoured cheque: LT Southon	339		6,281	Cr

The business's cash book (bank columns) for the same period was as follows.

BOOKS OF RIVERFORD WHOLESALE							
CASH BOOK (Bank columns only)							
Dr							Cr
Nov	1	Balance	4,155	Nov	1	KLK Ltd (chq 229203)	2,325
	7	Sales	4,782		3	Electricity (chq 229204)	1,012
	20	Sales	2,514		12	Admin expenses (chq 229205)	540
	20	M Lall	600		23	Westby Traders (chq 229206)	1,336
	28	Sales	3,724		26	H Taylor (chq 229207)	1,064
					27	Rent (standing order)	665
					31	Balance c/d	8,833
			15,775				15,775
Dec	1	Balance b/d	8,833				

(a) Update the cash book balance at 4 December 2011.

(b) Prepare a bank reconciliation statement dated 4 December 2011.

(c) Explain the benefits that arise for a business from the preparation of bank reconciliation statements.

2   The bank statement and cash book (bank columns) for August 2011 have been made available by Kylie Stephens, the owner of Newford Furniture.

SECURE BANK plc						
Bank Statement for NEWFORD FURNITURE						
Date		Details	Dr	Cr	Balance	
			£	£	£	
August	1	Balance			5,670	Dr
	7	Credit transfer: Homeware Retail		1,490	4,180	Dr
	9	107833 Endale Textiles	2,970		7,150	Dr
	11	DD Regional Telecoms plc	872		8,022	Dr
	15	CHR	103		8,125	Dr
	19	107837	675		8,800	Dr
	22	Sundry credit		3,379	5,421	Dr

| | 26 | 107834 | | 386 | | 5,807 | Dr |
| | 28 | SO Newford Property Rentals | | 775 | | 6,582 | Dr |

The business's cash book (bank columns) for the same period was as follows.

						BOOKS OF BEST FURNISHINGS	
						CASH BOOK (Bank columns only)	
Dr							Cr
Aug	17	Sales	3,379	Aug	1	Balance	5,670
	28	Sales	5,022		3	Endale Textiles (chq 107833)	2,970
	31	Balance c/d	4,403		8	General expenses (chq 107834)	386
					9	Business rates (chq 107835)	715
					12	Tower furniture plc (chq 107836)	1,440
					13	Drawings (chq 107837)	675
					24	Lakeford Ltd (chq 107838)	948
			12,804				12,804
				Sept	1	Balance b/d	4,403

(a) Update the cash book balance at 5 September 2011.

(b) Prepare a bank reconciliation statement dated 5 September 2011.

3   On 31 May 2011, Luigi Nono received a bank statement for his business which showed a closing balance which differed from that recorded in his cash book. On this date the cash book balance was overdrawn £724.

The following discrepancies between the two records were found:

- The bank statement showed a credit transfer of £840 from a customer, Supaford Ltd, which had not been recorded in the cash book.
- A standing order payment of £623 for rent had not yet been recorded in the cash book.
- A cheque sent to a supplier, Robin Lang, for £1,778, did not appear on the bank statement.
- Bank charges of £119 had been omitted from the cash book.
- The bank had yet to record cash sales of £1,823 paid in on 29 May 2011

(a) Update Luigi Nono's cash book balance on 31 May 2011.

(b) Prepare a bank reconciliation statement dated 31 May 2011 which shows the original balance shown on the bank statement received on this date.

3 Sales and purchases ledger control accounts

In this topic you will learn:

- the role, presentation and limitations of control accounts
- how to produce a sales ledger control account and a purchase ledger control account.

Sales and purchases ledger control accounts – structure

A control account is a 'master' total account and its purpose is to verify the accuracy of entries made in the subsidiary ledgers.

Remember, control accounts do NOT form part of the double entry system – they are effectively memorandum accounts.

When individual postings are made to the suppliers' accounts in the purchase ledger and the customers' accounts in the sales ledger, the totals of these postings may be transferred to the purchase ledger control account and sales ledger control account respectively.

In this way, the balance on the two control accounts should agree with the totals of the individual balances in the respective ledgers.

The structure of a typical **sales ledger control account** is as follows:

Dr						Cr
Date	Details	£	Date	Details		£
1 Nov	Balance b/d	80,000	30 Nov	Bank		93,000
30 Nov	Sales day book	102,000	30 Nov	Discounts allowed		2,000
30 Nov	Returned cheques	500	30 Nov	Sales returns day book		1,000
			30 Nov	Contras		1,500
			30 Nov	Bad debts written off		1,000
			30 Nov	Balance c/d		84,000
		182,500				182,500
1 Dec	Balance b/d	84,000				

Figure 3.3 *Sales ledger control account*

Guidance notes

1 **Balance b/d.** The total of all individual customer account balances at 1 November.
2 **Sales day book.** The total column in the sales day book.
3 **Returned cheques.** The total of all customer returned cheques in the period.
4 **Bank.** The total of all customer cheques and cash received in respect of credit sales only, from the cash book.
5 **Discounts allowed.** The total of the discounts allowed column from the debit side of the cash book.
6 **Sales returns day book.** The total column in the sales returns day book.
7 **Contras.** The total of all amounts set off against the purchases ledger accounts.
8 **Bad debts written off.** The total of all customer accounts that have been written off as bad debts in the period.
9 **Balance c/d.** The total of all individual customer account balances at 30 November.

Note

If any customer accounts have a credit balance rather than a debit balance, the total of these credit balances will be shown separately in the control account.

The structure of a typical purchases ledger control account is as follows:

Dr						Cr
Date	Details	£	Date	Details		£
30 Nov	Bank	66,000	1 Nov	Balance b/d		56,000
30 Nov	Discounts received	1,700	30 Nov	Purchases day book		72,000
30 Nov	Purchases returns day book	2,000	30 Nov	Cancelled cheques		1,200
30 Nov	Contras	1,500				
30 Nov	Balance c/d	58,000				
		129,200				129,200
			1 Dec	Balance b/d		58,000

Figure 3.4 *Purchases ledger control account*

Guidance notes

1 **Balance b/d.** The total of all individual supplier account balances at 1 November.
2 **Purchases day book.** The total column in the purchases day book.
3 **Cancelled cheques.** The total of all cheques drawn in favour of suppliers, but cancelled in the period.
4 **Bank.** The total of all supplier cheques and cash paid in respect of credit purchases only, from the cash book.
5 **Discounts received.** The total of the discounts received column from the credit side of the cash book.
6 **Purchases returns day book.** The total column in the purchases returns day book.
7 **Contras.** The total of all amounts set off against sales ledger accounts.
8 **Balance c/d.** The total of all individual supplier account balances at 30 November.

Note

If any supplier accounts have a debit balance rather than a credit balance, the total of these debit balances will be shown separately in the control account.

Key terms

Cancelled cheque: a cheque drawn by the business and subsequently cancelled before payment.

Contra entry: a cancellation of a debit balance with a credit balance in different books of account.

Returned cheque: a cheque that has been paid into the bank, but not honoured by the drawer's bank (usually because of lack of funds)

Activity

Explain the meaning of a contra in a purchases or sales ledger control account

Activity

Prepare a sales ledger control account for the month of April 2012 using the following information. The balance on the account should be entered as the closing balance at 30 April 2012.

	£
Sales ledger balances (debit) at 1 April 2012	66,480
Total of sales day book for April 2012	38,740
Total of sales returns day book for April 2012	614
Cash received from credit customers	44,594
Cash discounts allowed	379
Bad debts written off	125

Writing off bad debts in the sales ledger

There will be occasions when receivables are unable to pay what is owing to the business. Perhaps the customer disputes the amount owing or perhaps they have become bankrupt. These debts are then written off the customers' accounts in the sales ledger.

The process of writing off a bad debt in the sales ledger involves crediting the individual customer's account with the amount of the debt being written off.

Debit   Bad debts written off

Credit   Customer's account (in the sales ledger)

As we have seen, the control accounts do not form part of the double entry system, so in order to maintain the correct balance in the control account, the amount must also be posted to the credit of that account.

Illustration

How to prepare a purchases ledger control account

The following figures have been drawn from the books for the month ended 31 March 2012.

	£
Balances at 1 March 2012	
Credit balances	23,437
Debit balances	465
Balances at 31 March 2012	
Purchases on credit for the month	245,897
Returns to suppliers of credit purchases	4,679
Cash purchases	25,679
Purchases ledger balances set off against sales ledger	475
Cheques paid to suppliers	236,498
Discounts received	3,674
Cheque refunds from credit suppliers	450
Debit balance on the purchases ledger	749
Credit balances on the purchases ledger	?

Approach

In order to prepare the purchases ledger control account, the accountant must decide which, if any, of the items in this list do not belong in the purchases ledger control account.

The opening balance is known, but each other item should be taken in turn and a decision made as to whether it increases the balance owing or reduces it.

The final purchases ledger control account will be as follows, with the balancing figure representing the closing balances at 31 March. These could then be checked against the total of the list of balances extracted from the purchases ledger.

Dr				Purchases ledger control account			Cr
Date	Details	£	Date	Details	£		
1 March	Balances b/d	465	1 March	Balances b/d	23,437		
31 March	Returns outwards	4,679	31 March	Credit purchases	245,897		
31 March	Sales ledger contra	475	31 March	Bank	450		
31 March	Bank	236,498	31 March	Balances c/d	749		
31 March	Discounts received	3,674					
31 March	Balances c/d	24,742					
		270,533			270,533		
1 April	Balances b/d	749	1 April	Balances b/d	24,742		

Activity

The sales ledger control account for the month ended 31 October 2011 did not agree with the sales ledger balances list total.

The following errors have been discovered:

1 The sales day book was undercast by £540.

2 The returns inwards day book includes £100 that is actually for returns outwards.

3 A discount allowed of £37 has been omitted from the books completely.

4 A cheque received from J C Cross Garages for £1,479 was entered in the account of A B Cross Ltd in error.

5 The opening balance brought down should have been £25,080.

Enter the necessary corrections in the control account below and balance the account.

Dr			Sales ledger control account		Cr
Date	Details	£	Date	Details	£
31 Oct	Balance b/d	25,800			

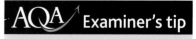

AQA Examiner's tip

The details column is very important when producing accounts. In a previous examiner's report, the principal examiner commented that details produced by candidates answering this question were at best 'sketchy'.

Benefits of control accounts

Accuracy

A balanced control account verifies the arithmetical accuracy of the subsidiary ledger.

Prevention of fraud

Control accounts should be maintained by a supervisor or member of staff other than the ledger clerk with responsibility for a particular ledger. As such, this segregation of duties acts as a deterrent to fraud and makes the discovery of fraud much easier.

Management information

Management are able to view a total amount owing from customers or owing to suppliers at any time, without totalling all of the individual accounts.

Preparation of financial statements

Having a control account balance enables interim or financial statements to be drawn up more quickly.

AQA Examiner's tip

Remember, a control account does not prove that individual balances are correct; it verifies the arithmetical accuracy of the ledger as a whole.

Activity

Explain the benefits of using the sales ledger control account to verify records and give examples of errors that will be revealed by the control account.

Explain the main limitation of control accounts using two examples to illustrate your answer.

Link

For more information on control accounts, see *A2 Accounting*, Unit 3.

Limitations of control accounts

Individual account balances

A balanced control account verifies the **arithmetical** accuracy of the ledger; it does NOT prove that each individual account balance is correct. The following errors will not be identified.

- **Errors of omission.** Where a transaction has been completely omitted from the records.
- **Compensating error.** Where equal and opposite errors cancel each other out.
- **Error of commission.** Where an amount is posted to an incorrect account of the correct type. For example Andrew Smith account instead of Alf Smith account.
- **Error of original entry.** Where an error is made transferring an amount from the source document into the book of original entry.

Learning outcomes

As a result of studying this topic, you should now be able to:

- state the purpose and importance of control accounts
- prepare a sales ledger control account and a purchases ledger control account
- comment on the benefits and limitations of control accounts

AQA Examination Style Questions

1 The following information was taken from the books of Desorada Brothers on 30 June 2011.

	£
total of receivables (debtors) balances on 1 June	8,370
total of sales day book	32,995
total receipts from cash book	27,348
total discounts allowed	1,892
total of returns inwards book	4,339
total bad debts from general journal	473

(a) Prepare the sales ledger control account for June 2011.
    The sales ledger clerk reported that the total of receivables (debtors) balances on 30 June 2011 was £7,313.
(b) Using your answer to (a), comment on the information provided by the sales ledger clerk.

2   The following information is to be entered in a purchases ledger control account for October 2011.

	£
Purchases ledger balances at 1 October 2011	
debit	370
credit	29,772
Totals for the month:	
credit purchases	94,571
returns outwards	4,489
payments to payables	81,338
discounts received	1,983
interest charged on overdue accounts	175
Contra (credit balance in purchases ledger transferred to the sales ledger)	847
Purchases ledger balances at 31 October 2011	
debit	484
credit	?

3   Carla is responsible for preparing purchases ledger and sales ledger control accounts at the end of each month. On 31 January 2012, Carla had extracted the following information from the business's accounting records.

	£
Balances at 1 January 2012	
sales ledger debit balance	19,810
sales ledger credit balance	272
purchases ledger debit balance	394
purchases ledger credit balance	14,770
Sales	
credit sales	63,660
cash sales	19,400
Purchases	
credit purchases	43,376
cash purchases	2,664
Payments to trade payables	41,720
Receipts from trade receivables	64,847
Returns inwards (from returns inwards day book)	1,349
Returns outwards (from returns outwards day book)	668
Bad debts (sales ledger accounts written off)	823
Discounts allowed	703
Discounts received	994
Interest charged on the overdue accounts of receivables	211
Contra entry (debit balance in sales ledger transferred to purchase ledger)	658
Balances at 31 January 2012	
sales ledger debit balance	?
sales ledger credit balance	227
purchases ledger debit balance	484
purchases ledger credit balance	?

Prepare a purchases ledger control account and sales ledger control account for January 2012. Select the relevant information from the information provided.

4   David Roberts prepared the following sales ledger control on 28 February 2012.

Dr						Sales Ledger Control Account		Cr
Feb	1	Opening balance	13,792	Feb	1	Opening balance		392
	28	Sales	88,731		28	Returns inwards		3,721
	28	Balance c/d	139		28	Receipts		79,774
					28	Discounts allowed		2,316
					28	Bad debts		882
					28	Closing balance c/d		15,577
			102,662					102,662
Mar	1	Balance b/d	15,577	Mar	1	Balance b/d		139

However, David has now discovered the following errors had been made when preparing this account.

1   The figure for sales includes cash sales of £14,302.
2   A cheque for £1,069 received from a credit customer in settlement of his account had been banked in early February and this was correctly recorded in the books of account. However, David had overlooked the fact that the bank had returned this cheque.
3   The total bad debts for February should have been recorded as £828.
4   A credit balance in the purchases ledger had been transferred to the sales ledger in February 2012. This item had been omitted from the sales ledger control account.

(a) Prepare a corrected version of the sales ledger control account.
(b) Explain why control accounts do not reveal all the errors which can occur in the personal ledgers. Illustrate your answer with a suitable example.

4 Financial statements

The final chapter in Unit 1 brings together all of the information that has been processed so far in the preparation of the end-of-year financial statements of the business.

The financial statements comprise two main statements:

- The income statement (which consists of a trading section and a profit and loss section)
- The statement of financial position (balance sheet).

Having learned how to produce the trial balance, the final step is to prepare an income statement with a section to identify the gross profit and a profit and loss section to identify the profit; plus a statement of financial position (balance sheet) to provide a statement of the business's capital, assets and liabilities at a given date.

You will also learn in this final chapter how to make simple adjustments to the final accounts in respect of:

- Closing inventory
- Prepayments
- Accruals
- Bad debts
- Depreciation.

These adjustments are an introduction to an important area of study that will be further developed in Unit 2. If the financial statements were not adjusted for the items listed above, they would not represent an accurate reflection of either the profit or loss, or of the state of the business's affairs at a given date (the true and fair view).

1 The income statement and statement of financial position (balance sheet)

The starting point for the preparation of the financial statement is the trial balance, listing all of the balances from the general ledger.

Income statement (trading section)

The trading section of the income statement compares sales for the period with the **cost of sales** for the period. The difference between these two figures is the **gross profit**. Nowadays, it is usual to find the term 'revenue' used in financial statements instead of sales.

- the nature and purpose of the trading section of the income statement

- the nature and purpose of the profit and loss section of the income statement

- the nature and purpose of the statement of financial position (balance sheet)

- how to prepare the income statement and statement of financial position (balance sheet) from the trial balance.

Background knowledge

The financial statements of a business will be prepared annually as a matter of course, but more frequently (perhaps monthly or quarterly) to inform management on how the business is performing.

AQA Examiner's tip

Returns inwards should be deducted from sales and **returns outwards** should be deducted from purchases.

Key terms

Cost of sales: the total purchases plus carriage inwards and returns outwards adjusted for opening and closing inventory.

Gross profit: the difference between sales and the cost of those sales.

Link

For more information on inventory valuation, see Chapter 6, page 88.

The format for a trading section is shown in Figure 4.1.

	£	£	£
Revenue			XXX
Less: returns inwards			(XXX)
			XXX
Cost of sales			
Opening inventory		XXX	
Purchases	XXX		
Less : returns outwards	(XXX)		
	XXX		
Add: Carriage inwards	XXX	XXX	
		XXX	
Less: Closing inventory		(XXX)	XXX
Gross profit			XXX

Figure 4.1 *Trading section*

Adjustment for inventory in the trading section of the income statement

The value of inventory that is included in the trial balance is always the opening inventory. The value of closing inventory will appear as additional information after the trial balance.

As we have seen, to maintain the principles of double entry, every debit must have an equal credit. In order to adhere to this rule, the value of closing inventory will be as follows:

Debit: **Current assets in the statement of financial position (balance sheet).** (Inventory is an asset that the business holds at the end of the accounting period.)

Credit: **Trading section of income statement.** (Inventory still held by the business reduces the cost of sales.)

Activity

Cost of revenue (in end of year financial statements)

Calculate the cost of revenue (in end of year financial statements) from the following figures

Opening inventory	35,000
Purchases	165,300
Returns outwards	1,800
Carriage inwards	3,400
Closing inventory	32,000

Activity

Preparing a trading section of an income statement

The following information has been extracted from the books of account of A Tate at 31 August 2011.

	£
Carriage inwards	3,763
Carriage outwards	4,078
Discounts allowed	4,221
Discounts received	**2,089**
Drawings	38,410
Inventory at 1 September 2010	75,840
Inventory at 31 August 2011	62,706
Purchases	212,438
Returns inwards	8,444
Returns outwards	6,204
Revenue	356,270
Shop expenses	37,555

Prepare the trading section of the income statement for the year ended 31 August 2011.

Key terms

Profit: the final figure in the income statement when the gross profit is *greater than* the expenses that have been deducted from it.

Loss: the final figure in the income statement when the gross profit is *less than* the expenses that have been deducted from it.

Profit and loss section of income statement

The profit and loss section of the income statement commences with the gross profit brought down from the trading section, adds any other income, (for example discounts received, rents received, etc.) and deducts the expenses of running the business during the period.

If income is greater than expenditure, then a **profit** results, but if expenditure is greater than income, then a **loss** results.

A typical profit and loss section would appear as follows

AQA Examiner's tip

The heading for an income statement should always be given in full. Example: Income statement for the year ended 31 December 2011. Make a point of avoiding any abbreviations.

	£	£
Gross profit		XXX
Add: Discounts received		XXX
		XXX
Less: expenses		
Carriage outwards	XXX	
Discounts allowed	XXX	
Motor expenses	XXX	
Office expenses	XXX	
Stationery and advertising	XXX	
		(XXX)
Profit for the year		XXX

Figure 4.2 *Profit and loss section*

Link

For more information on profit and loss sections, see Chapter 7, page 97.

Statement of financial position (balance sheet)

The statement of financial position (balance sheet) is a statement prepared at the end of an accounting period, summarising the capital account of the owner of the business and detailing the assets and liabilities representing that capital investment on a specific date.

It is important to analyse assets and liabilities under the correct sub-headings.

Non-current assets are intended to be held for more than one financial period. They are not purchased with the intention of being resold; the intention is that they should be held to generate profits for the business.

Examples of non-current assets are premises, motor vehicles, machinery, etc.

Current assets are cash or assets that will be turned into cash within the next twelve months. Current assets should be listed in reverse **order of liquidity** on the statement of financial position (balance sheet), starting with the least liquid (inventory) down to the most liquid (cash).

Examples of current assets are closing inventories, receivables, prepayments, cash at bank (sometimes referred to as cash and cash equivalents).

Current liabilities are amounts owed by the business in the short term that will be paid within the next twelve months.

Examples of current liabilities are payables, accruals and bank overdrafts.

Net current assets/liabilities is the difference between current assets and current liabilities.

Non-current liabilities are amounts owed by the business that are not due to be paid in the next twelve months.

Examples of non-current liabilities are bank loans and mortgages.

Capital account is the amount of the investment in the business made by the owner. The capital account on the statement of financial position (balance sheet) is represented as follows:

	£
Balance brought forward *(from the previous year's statement of financial position (balance sheet))*.	XXX
Add: Capital introduced during the year.	XXX
Add: Profit for the year *or*	XXX
Deduct: Loss for the year	(XXX)
	XXX
Deduct: Drawings.	(XXX)
Balance carried forward *(to the next year's statement of financial position (balance sheet))*	XXX

Figure 4.3 *Capital account*

The closing balance on the capital account will always be equal to and represented by the excess of assets over liabilities.

This conforms to the accounting equation:

$$\text{Assets} - \text{Liabilities} = \text{Capital}$$

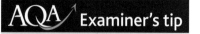

Link

For more information on financial statements, see Chapter 7, page 90.

Activity

Explain the difference between:

- Current assets and current assets. Give one example of a current asset and one example of a non-current asset.
- Current liabilities and non-current liabilities.

Step by step guide to preparing financial statements from a trial balance

1 Identify on the trial balance items for the trading section of the income statement, items for the profit and loss section of the income statement and items for the statement of financial position (balance sheet) and mark these on the trial balance against each heading.
2 Draft the income statement heading.
3 Transfer all relevant amounts into the trading section and calculate the gross profit.
4 Open the profit and loss section with the gross profit brought down from the trading section.
5 Transfer all relevant amounts into the profit and loss section and calculate the profit or loss.
6 Draft the statement of financial position (balance sheet) headings.
7 Transfer all remaining amounts into the statement of financial position (balance sheet).

Case study

CK Traders

Chris Knight is an ex-professional footballer. When he retired from playing football two years ago, he set up his own business, CK Traders selling sportswear.

Illustration

How to prepare a trading and an income statement

Chris Knight's bookkeeper has extracted the following trial balance at 31 May 2011:

	Dr (£)	Cr (£)
Capital account at 1 June 2010		46,960
Carriage inwards	1,650	
Carriage outwards	1,130	
Cash at bank	2,100	
Discounts allowed	680	
Discounts received		1,450
Drawings	23,200	
Inventory at 1 June 2010		43,000
Mortgage on premises (repayable 2013)	32,400	
Motor expenses	3,480	
Motor vehicle at cost	18,000	

 Examiner's tip

To avoid common errors, note:

- The **inventory** shown on the trial balance is the **opening inventory**.
- The **closing inventory** is shown as a separate note after the trial balance and appears in both the income statement and the statement of financial position (balance sheet) to complete the double entry.
- Carriage inwards appears in the trading section; carriage outwards appears in the profit and loss section. Both are expenses (debit balances).
- Drawings appear as a deduction from the capital account. They do not appear in income statement.
- Discounts received appear AFTER the gross profit.
- Don't forget to show the complete heading in the income statement **with no abbreviations**.
- Show all relevant workings.

	Dr	Cr
Office expenses	8,410	
Premises at cost	75,000	
Purchases	190,340	
Returns inwards	800	
Returns outwards		400
Revenue		256,200
Stationery and advertising	2,370	
Trade payables		32,350
Trade receivables	20,800	
Totals	**380,360**	**380,360**

Additional information
Inventory at 31 May 2011 is £28,150

Required

Chris needs to prepare an income statement for CK Traders for the year ended 31 May 2011 and a statement of financial position (balance sheet) at that date.

Step 1 Identify on the trial balance items for the trading section, items for the profit and loss section and items for the statement of financial position (balance sheet) and mark this on the trial balance against each heading.

	Dr (£)	Cr (£)	Working
Capital account at 1 June 2010		46,960	*Balance sheet*
Carriage inwards	1,650		*Trading*
Carriage outwards	1,130		*Profit & loss*
Cash at bank	2,100		*Balance sheet*
Discounts allowed	680		*Profit & loss*
Discounts received		1,450	*Profit & loss*
Drawings	23,200		*Balance sheet*
Inventory at 1 June 2010	32,400		*Trading*
Mortgage on premises (repayable 2013)		43,000	*Balance sheet*
Motor expenses	3,480		*Profit & loss*
Motor vehicle at cost	18,000		*Balance sheet*
Office expenses	8,410		*Profit & loss*
Premises at cost	75,000		*Balance sheet*
Purchases	190,340		*Trading*
Returns inwards	800		*Trading*
Returns outwards		400	*Trading*

Revenue		256,200	Trading
Stationery and advertising	2,370		Profit & loss
Trade payables		32,350	Balance sheet
Trade receivables	20,800		Balance sheet
Totals	**380,360**	**380,360**	

Analysed trial balance

Step 2 Draft the income statement.

Step 3 Transfer all relevant amounts onto the trading account and calculate the gross profit.

CK Traders
Income statements for the year ended 31 May 2011

	£	£	£
Revenue			256,200
Less: returns inwards			800
			255,400
Cost of sales			
Inventory at 1 June 2010		32,400	
Purchases	190,340		
Less: returns outwards	400		
	189,940		
Carriage inwards	1,650	191,590	
		223,990	
Less: Inventory at 31 May 2011		28,150	195,840
Gross profit			**59,560**
Add: Discounts received			1,450
			61,010
Less: expenses			
Carriage outwards		1,130	
Discounts allowed		680	
Motor expenses		3,480	
Office expenses		8,410	
Stationery and advertising		2,370	
			16,070
Profit for the year			**44,940**

Step 4 Open the profit and loss section with the gross profit brought down from the trading section.

Step 5 Transfer all relevant amounts into the profit and loss section and calculate the profit or loss.

CK Traders.
Statement of financial position (balance sheet) at 31 May 2011

	£	£
Non-current assets		
Premises at cost	75,000	
Motor vehicles at cost	18,000	93,000

Step 6 Draft the statement of financial position (balance sheet) headings.

Current assets		
Inventory	28,150	
Trade receivables	20,800	
Cash at bank	2,100	
	51,050	
Less Current liabilities		
Trade payables	32,350	
Net current assets		18,700
		111,700
Less Non-current liabilities		
Mortgage on premises (repayable 2013)		43,000
		68,700
Capital account		
Brought forward at 1 June 2010		46,960
Add: Profit for the year		44,940
		91,900
Deduct: Drawings		23,200
		68,700

Step 7 Transfer all remaining amounts into the statement of financial position (balance sheet).

Examiner's tip

Clearly label the sub headings – 'Non-current assets', 'Current assets', 'Current liabilities'. 'Non-current liabilities' and 'Capital account'.

Learning outcomes

As a result of studying this topic, you should now be able to:

- describe the structure of the income statement and the statement of financial position (balance sheet)
- prepare the headings and sub-headings in the financial statements
- prepare the financial statements

AQA Examination Style Questions

1   Estellita Cameron owns 'In the Pink', a health food business. The following trial balance was extracted from the business's books of account on 31 December 2011.

Trial Balance at 31 December 2011		
	£	£
Bank loan (repayable March 2012)		3,000
Bank overdraft		1,743
Capital		374,525
Carriage inwards	1,378	
Carriage outwards	882	

Discounts allowed	1,085	
Discounts received		737
Drawings	29,900	
Insurance	4,489	
Inventory at 1 January 2011	25,507	
Loan interest	486	
Non-current assets	345,000	
Purchases	157,284	
Repairs and maintenance	474	
Returns inwards	1,881	
Returns outwards		2,390
Revenue		234,310
Trade payables		14,720
Trade receivables	5,118	
Wages and salaries	57,204	
Suspense account	737	
	631,525	631,525

Additional information

The business's inventory of unsold goods on 31 December 2011 was valued at £17,983

Estellita found that the difference in the trial balance totals was caused by the failure to post the total of the returns inwards book for December to the general ledger.

Prepare the following:
(a) income statement for the year ended 31 December 2011
(b) statement of financial position (balance sheet) at 31 December 2011.

2   Rakesh owns 'Rakesh's Taxis'. His business's financial year ended on 31 January 2012 when the following balances were extracted from his business's books of account.

	£
Bank loan (repayable 2015)	20,000
Bank overdraft	3,722
Capital	174,386
Cash in hand	729
Drawings	33,450
Drivers' wages	89,470
Furniture and equipment	16,500
Insurance	18,227
Office expenses	3,462
Loan interest	858
Rent	19,470
Revenue (receipts from customers)	169,870

Trade payables	911
Trade receivables	483
Vehicle fuel charges	24,558
Vehicle repairs	5,682
Vehicles	156,000
	411,300

Prepare an income statement for the year ended 31 January 2012 and a statement of financial position (balance sheet) at that date.

The financial statements we have produced so far, have all been produced directly from the closing balances from the general ledger, found in the trial balance. In reality, because the accounts are not drawn up on a cash basis, adjustments will need to be made to some of these figures to account for depreciation, bad debts, accruals and prepayments.

Depreciation

Depreciation is the apportionment of the **cost** of an asset over its **estimated useful economic life**. The value of a non-current asset falls due to age, wear and tear, obsolescence, etc. The charge for depreciation appears as an expense in the profit and loss section of the income statement and represents the cost to the business of using that asset over the financial period.

Note: the only non-current asset that does not depreciate is land since this has an infinite life.

There are a number of different methods of calculating depreciation, but the only one studied in this unit is the straight-line method.

Straight-line depreciation involves spreading the **net cost** of the asset over its estimated useful economic life.

$$\text{Depreciation for the year} = \frac{\text{Cost} - \text{estimated residual value}}{\text{Estimated useful economic life}}$$

Key terms

Cost: the price paid for the asset.

Estimated useful economic life: the estimated time that the business will continue to use the asset.

Net cost: initial cost of the asset less the estimated residual value at the end of the asset's useful economic life.

Estimated residual value: the estimated value of the asset at the end of its useful life.

Illustration

How to calculate annual charge for depreciation

Mohammed purchases new machinery for £28,000 and estimates that its useful life will be 5 years. Mohammed estimates that the machinery will be worth £3,000 at the end of five years. Calculate the annual charge for depreciation to appear in Mohammed's final accounts for the year.

Initial cost	£28,000
Estimated residual value	£ 3,000
Net cost	£25,000

The net cost of £25,000 will be spread over the useful economic life of 5 years.

Working: £25,000/5 years = £5,000 per annum.

Accounting entries for depreciation

As with all accounting entries, we must maintain the principles of double entry. As already stated, the value of assets fall as they depreciate and to take account of this reduction in value, an account is opened for provision for depreciation account, representing the accumulated depreciation of the asset. At the end of the financial year, the provision for depreciation account is credited with the charge for depreciation for the year.

Dr   Depreciation (income statement)

Cr   Provision for depreciation account

When completing the financial statements, the credit balance on the provision for depreciation account is deducted from the non-current asset at cost account to leave a net book value of the asset appearing on the statement of financial position (balance sheet) (see the illustration below).

*Note: Candidates will **not** be required to make ledger account entries for depreciation.*

Link

For more information on depreciation, see Chapter 7, page 103.

■ Illustration

A trial balance and statement of financial position (balance sheet)

Trial balance (extract)

	Dr (£)	Cr (£)
Motor vehicle cost	18,000	
Motor vehicle provision for depreciation		6,000

Statement of financial position (balance sheet) (extract)

Non-current assets	(£)	(£)
Motor vehicle cost	18,000	
Motor vehicle provision for depreciation	6,000	12,000

AQA Examiner's tip

An examination question may state that depreciation is to be calculated at 10% per annum using the straight-line method.

In these circumstances, the depreciation charge for the year will be 10% of the cost of the asset.

■ Activity

Depreciation

Martin purchases new machinery at a cost of £12,400. He estimates that the useful life of the machinery will be five years and that at the end of five years it will have a net realisable value of £400.

1 Calculate the annual depreciation charge using the straight-line method of depreciation.

2 Calculate the book value of the machinery at the end of three years.

Link

For more information on bad debts, see Chapter 7, page 90.

Bad debt write off

As we have seen in the section on control accounts, there will be occasions when receivables are unable to pay what is owing to the business. Perhaps the customer disputes the amount owing or perhaps they have become bankrupt. These debts are then written off the customers' accounts in the sales ledger. This write off is an expense to the business and must therefore be charged in the profit and loss section of income statements, so that the financial statements reflect the correct position.

If we fail to write off a debt that is not going to be recovered, the effect will be twofold.

1 The profit will be overstated by the amount of the bad debt, and

2 The statement of financial position (balance sheet) will not reflect the correct position – receivables will be overstated by the amount of the bad debt.

AQA Examiner's tip

If you are provided with a trial balance that includes a debit balance for bad debts, this will simply be recorded in the profit and loss section of the same income statements as an expense.

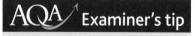

Illustration

How to include a bad debt in the income statement

Bob has produced a trial balance that includes the following figure:

	Dr (£)	Cr (£)
Bad debts written off	516	

The fact that this amount is already in the trial balance shows that the debt has already been written off.

Action: Include the £516 as an expense in the profit and loss section of the income statement. No further action is required.

You may be given an instruction to write off a particular bad debt. In these circumstances, you will record the bad debt in the profit and loss section of the income statement as an expense and also reduce receivables by the same amount. In other words:

Debit   Bad debts written off (income statement)

Credit   Receivables (statement of financial position (balance sheet))

Illustration

How to increase bad debts written off and reduce receivables

Chris has produced a trial balance that includes the following figures:

	Dr (£)	Cr (£)
Bad debts written off	120	
Receivables	12,500	

You are told that a debt outstanding from David of £350 is outstanding, but will not be paid because David is now bankrupt. Write off the debt outstanding from David.

You are given a clear instruction to write off the bad debt.

Action: Increase bad debts written off by £350 and reduce receivables by £350. The amounts to appear in the financial statements will be as follows:

Bad debts written off £470 (£120 + £350)

Receivables £12,150 (£12,500 – £350)

Accrual of expenses

An accrual is a liability for services that have already been used, but that have not yet been invoiced to the business.

To account for accruals in the financial statements

- Increase the expense charge from the trial balance by the amount of the accrual.
- Include the amount of the accrual in the statement of financial position (balance sheet) as a current liability.

Activity

Detail the bookkeeping entries required to write off a bad debt and state the effect that writing off a bad debt will have on the profit for the year.

■ Illustration

How to accrue expenses

Anna has produced a trial balance at 30 May 2011 that includes the following figure:

	Dr (£)	Cr (£)
Electricity	1,430	

You are told that Anna has used £150 electricity that has not yet been billed. Provide an accrual for this amount.

Action: Increase electricity by £150, the amount that has been used but not yet billed and include the accrual on the statement of financial position (balance sheet) as a current liability

In this way, the charge for electricity in the profit and loss section of the income statement will be £1,580, representing the amount of electricity actually used.

To account for accruals

Using the above illustration, the entry to account for the accrual is as follows:

Debit   Electricity   £150

Credit   Accruals   £150

Since the accrual of £150 is to be carried forward into the next accounting period, the ledger account will appear as follows:

Dr			Electricity			Cr
Date	Details	£	Date	Details		£
31 May	Balance (trial balance)	1,430	31 May	Income statement		1,580
31 May	Balance c/d	150				
		1,580				1,580
			1 June	Balance b/d		150

■ Activity

Accruals

Marion has prepared a trial balance at 30 June 2011, but has now been told that an accrual is required for £350 in respect of telephone charges. Enter the accrual in the telephone charges account below and close off the account by transferring the correct amount to the income statement.

Dr			Telephone charges			Cr
Date	Details	£	Date	Details		£
30 June	Balance b/d	3,495				
		___				___
		___				___

Prepayment of expenses

A prepayment arises when an expense is paid in advance and all or part of the payment relates to the next accounting period.

To account for prepayments in the financial statements.

■ Reduce the expense charge from the trial balance by the amount of the prepayment.

■ Include the amount of the prepayment in the statement of financial position (balance sheet) as a current asset.

Illustration

How to calculate a prepayment

Adit has produced a trial balance that includes the following figure:

	Dr (£)	Cr (£)
Rates	2,400	

You are told that Adit paid £2,400 for rates in April 2011 for the twelve months ending 31 March 2012. Adit is now preparing his final accounts for the year ending 31 December 2011. Calculate the amount of the prepayment for rates and provide for this in the final accounts.

Action: The amount of rates for the current accounting period is £2,400/12 months × 9 months (the nine months from April 2011 to December 2011). Therefore three months (January 2012 to March 2012) are paid in advance. The amount of the prepayment is £2,400 / 12 months × 3 months = £600.

To process the prepayment, decrease rates by £600 and include the prepayment of £600 on the statement of financial position (balance sheet) as a current asset.

In this way, the charge for rates in the income statement will be £1,800 representing the nine-months charge relating to the current financial year.

To account for prepayments

Using the above illustration, the entry to account for the prepayment is as follows:

Debit	Prepayments	£600
Credit	Rates	£600

Since the prepayment of £600 is to be carried forward into the next accounting period, the ledger account will appear as follows:

Dr			Rates			Cr
Date	Details	£	Date	Details		£
30 April	Bank	2,400	31 Dec	Income statement		1,800
			31 Dec	Balance c/d		600
		2,400				2,400
1 Jan	Balance b/d	600				

Link

For more information on adjustments, see Chapter 7, page 92.

Activity

Accruals and prepayments

Tom is preparing his accounts for the year ended 30 September 2011. On 1 January 2011, he made the following payments

	£
Rent (£300 per month)	2,400
Rates (£250 per quarter)	1,000

Calculate

- The charge to appear in the income statement for rent and rates.
- The amounts to appear on the statement of financial position (balance sheet) for accruals and prepayments.

Case study

Northern Sports

Northern Sports is a wholesale business supplying sportswear based in Leicester. The business was started five years ago by Cheryl McGowan and has gone from strength to strength as personal fitness has become more important to people's lifestyles.

Illustration

How to deal with adjustments

Cheryl's bookkeeper has extracted the following trial balance at 30 June 2011 and supplied the additional information as detailed.

	Dr (£)	Cr (£)
Bank overdraft		15,443
Capital account at 1 July 2010		76,961
Carriage inwards	2,701	
Carriage outwards	2,465	
Discounts allowed	1,190	
Discounts received		2,731
Drawings	26,475	
Heating and lighting	3,928	
Inventory at 1 July 2010	83,480	
Mortgage on premises (repayable 2015)		86,000
Motor expenses	8,435	
Motor vehicles at cost	36,400	
Office expenses	2,660	

Premises at cost	138,000	
Property repairs	2,085	
Provision for depreciation motor vehicles		7,280
Provision for depreciation shop fittings		5,680
Purchases	214,560	
Returns inwards	3,771	
Returns outwards		1,638
Revenue		412,804
Shop fittings at cost	28,400	
Trade payables		16,196
Trade receivables	33,772	
Wages and salaries	36,411	
Totals	**624,733**	**624,733**

Additional information

1 Inventory at 30 June 2011 was valued at £78,250.

2 Motor expenses were prepaid by £85.

3 Accrue £132 in respect of heating and lighting.

4 Depreciate motor vehicles at 25% using the straight-line method.

5 Depreciate shop fittings at 10% per annum using the straight-line method.

6 Write off bad debts of £382.

Approach

Step 1 Having identified where all of the trial balance items are to be allocated in the financial statements, deal with each of the adjustments in turn.

▨ The inventory at 30 June 2011 is a current asset on the statement of financial position (balance sheet) and will reduce the cost of sales in the trading section of the income statement.

▨ Dr Inventory (statement of financial position (balance sheet) current assets)

▨ Cr Inventory (trading section)

Step 2 The prepayment of £85 for motor expenses relates to the next accounting period. It will therefore reduce the charge for motor expenses this year and will be a current asset on the statement of financial position (balance sheet).

▨ Dr Prepayments (statement of financial position (balance sheet) current assets)

▨ Cr Motor expenses (profit and loss section of the income statement)

Step 3 The accrual of £132 for heating and lighting has not yet been invoiced to the business, but has been used and will therefore increase the charge for heating and lighting in the current accounting period and the amount owing will be a current liability on the statement of financial position (balance sheet).

▓ Dr Heating and lighting (profit and loss section of the income statement)

▓ Cr Accruals (statement of financial position (balance sheet) current liabilities)

Step 4 The annual depreciation charge for motor vehicles is to be calculated at 25% based on the cost of the assets.

£36,400 × 25% = £9,100. The charge for the year is an expense in the income statement and will increase the provision for depreciation on the statement of financial position (balance sheet).

▓ Dr Depreciation (income statement)

▓ Cr Provision for depreciation motor vehicles (statement of financial position (balance sheet))

Step 5 The annual depreciation charge for shop fittings is to be calculated at 10% based on the cost of the assets.

£28,400 × 10% = £2,840. The charge for the year is an expense in the income statement and will increase the provision for depreciation on the statement of financial position (balance sheet).

▓ Dr Depreciation (income statement)

▓ Cr Provision for depreciation shop fittings (statement of financial position (balance sheet))

Step 6 Writing off the bad debts of £382 is an expense in the income statement and will reduce receivables on the statement of financial position (balance sheet).

▓ Dr Bad debts (income statement)

▓ Cr Receivables (statement of financial position (balance sheet) current assets)

Working sheet

	Dr (£)	Cr (£)	Adjust Dr (£)	Adjust Cr (£)	
Bank overdraft		15,443			*Balance sheet*
Capital account at 1 July 2010		76,961			*Balance sheet*
Carriage inwards	2,701				*Trading account*
Carriage outwards	2,465				*Profit and loss*
Discounts allowed	1,190				*Profit and loss*
Discounts received		2,731			*Profit and loss*
Drawings	26,475				*Balance sheet*
Heating and lighting	3,928		132		*Profit and loss*
Inventory at 1 July 2010	83,480				*Trading*
Mortgage on premises (repayable 2015)		86,000			*Balance sheet*
Motor expenses	8,435			85	*Profit and loss*
Motor vehicles at cost	36,400				*Balance sheet*
Office expenses	2,660				*Profit and loss*
Premises at cost	138,000				*Balance sheet*

Property repairs	2,085				*Profit and loss*
Provision for depreciation motor vehicles		7,280		9,100	*Balance sheet*
Provision for depreciation shop fittings		5,680		2,840	*Balance sheet*
Purchases	214,560				*Trading account*
Returns inwards	3,771				*Trading account*
Returns outwards		1,638			*Trading account*
Revenue		412,804			*Trading account*
Shop fittings at cost	28,400				*Balance sheet*
Trade payables		16,196			*Balance sheet*
Trade receivables	33,772			382	*Balance sheet*
Wages and salaries	36,411				*Profit and loss*
Inventory at 30 June 2011 (trading)				78,250	*Trading account*
Inventory at 30 June 2011 (statement of financial position (balance sheet))			78,250		*Balance sheet*
Prepayments			85		*Balance sheet*
Accruals				132	*Balance sheet*
Depreciation (motor vehicles)			9,100		*Profit and loss*
Depreciation (shop fillings)			2,840		*Profit and loss*
Bad debts			382		*Profit and loss*
Totals	624,733	624,733	90,789	90,789	

Solution

Northern Sports

Income statement for the year ended 30 June 2011

	£	£	£
Revenue			412,804
Less: returns inwards			3,771
			409,033
Cost of sales			
Inventory at 1 July 2010		83,480	
Purchases	214,560		
Less: returns outwards	1,638		
	212,922		
Carriage inwards	2,701	215,623	
		299,103	
Less: Inventory at 30 June 2011		78,250	220,853
Gross profit			188,180
Add: Discounts received			2,731
			190,911
Less; expenses			
Bad debts		382	
Carriage outwards		2,465	
Depreciation		11,940	

Discounts allowed	1,190	
Heating and lighting	4,060	
Motor expenses	8,350	
Office expenses	2,660	
Property repairs	2,085	
Wages and salaries	36,411	
		69,543
Profit for the year		**121,368**

Northern Sports

Statement of financial position (balance sheet) at 30 June 2011

	£	£
NON-CURRENT ASSETS		
Premises at cost		138,000
Motor vehicles at cost	36,400	
Less: provision for depreciation	16,380	20,020
Shop fittings at cost	28,400	
Less: provision for depreciation	8,520	19,880
		177,900
CURRENT ASSETS		
Inventory	78,250	
Receivables	33,390	
Prepayments	85	
	111,725	
CURRENT LIABILITIES		
Payables	16,196	
Accruals	132	
Bank overdraft	15,443	
	31,771	
Net current assets		79,954
		257,854
NON-CURRENT LIABILITIES		
Mortgage on premises (repayable 2015)		86,000
		171,854
CAPITAL ACCOUNT		
Brought forward		76,961
Add: Profit for the year		121,368
		198,329
Deduct: Drawings		26,475
		171,854

Learning outcomes

As a result of studying this topic, you should now be able to:

- adjust financial statements to take account of closing inventory, accruals, prepayments, depreciation and bad debts written off

- process adjustments to an incorrect statement of financial position (balance sheet)

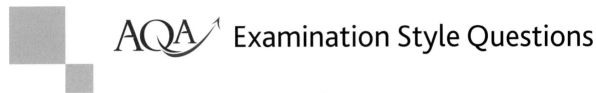

AQA Examination Style Questions

1   'Dexter Sports' is a retail unit opened two years ago by Alex Dexter. The following trial balance has been extracted from the business's books of account at end of the third year of trading.

Trial Balance at 31 December 2011		
	Dr	Cr
	£	£
Administration expenses	3,372	
Business rates	9,043	
Cash at bank	7,381	
Capital		40,373
Carriage outwards	465	
Drawings	31,860	
Furniture and fittings		
cost	30,000	
provision for depreciation at 1 January 2011		12,000
Insurance	3,668	
Inventory at 1 January 2011	28,420	
Purchases	204,364	
Rent	26,300	
Returns	1,704	2,946
Revenue		344,291
Trade payables		8,423
Trade receivables	3,227	
Vehicles		
cost	34,000	
provision for depreciation at 1 January 2011		17,000
Wages	41,229	
	425,033	425,033

Additional information:

1. The inventory on 31 December 2011 was valued at £25,270.

2. The following expenses were prepaid at 31 December 2011: business rates £495; insurance £176.

3. The following expenses were due but unpaid at 31 December 2011: administration expenses £292; rent £380.

4. The business's depreciation policy is as follows:
   - ■ furniture and fittings: is depreciated by 20% per annum using the straight-line method;
   - ■ vehicles: are depreciated by 25% per annum using the straight-line method.

Prepare the business's income statement for the year ended 31 December 2011 and a statement of financial position (balance sheet) at that date.

2. Trentford Wholesale is owned by Shamilla Spencer. The business's financial year ended on 31 October 2011. The trading section of the income statement had already been prepared when the following trial balance was extracted from the business's books.

	£	£
Bad debts written off	1,242	
Bank loan (repayable April 2012)		8,400
Business rates	12,750	
Capital		380,000
Cash at bank	8,391	
Discounts	581	727
Drawings	41,490	
Financial charges	1,089	
Freehold premises at cost		
cost	580,000	
provision for depreciation 1 November 2010		46,400
Furniture and equipment at cost		
cost	47,400	
provision for depreciation at 1 November 2010		21,330
General expenses	3,112	
Gross profit		457,500
Insurance	9,450	
Inventory at 1 November 2010	53,482	
Light and heat	8,372	
Selling and distribution costs	6,584	
Trade payables		17,019
Trade receivables	13,331	
Vehicle at cost	28,300	
Wages and salaries	115,802	
	931,376	931,376

Additional information

1 Business rates, £1,056, was prepaid at 31 October 2011.

2 Insurance includes a payment of £960 which covers the period 1 November 2011 to 31 January 2012.

3 Wages and salaries due but unpaid at 31 October 2011 totalled £3,910.

4 Shamilla has decided that the balance of trade receivable's account, £506, should now be written off as a bad debt.

5 Freehold premises should be depreciated by 2% per annum using the straight-line method; furniture and equipment should be depreciated by 15% per annum using the straight-line method.

6 The vehicle was purchased on 1 November 2010. It has been estimated that the vehicle will have a residual value of £5,700 at the end of its useful life. It has been decided to depreciate the vehicle over 4 years using the straight-line method.

Prepare:

(a) an income statement for the year ended 31 October 2011.

(b) a statement of financial position (balance sheet) at 31 October 2011.

3 The following trial balance was extracted from the books of Krishna Persad after the preparation of his business's income statement for the year ended 30 September 2011.

Trial Balance at 30 September 2011		
	£	£
Accruals		3,120
Bank loan (repayable August 2013)		14,300
Bank overdraft		2,759
Capital		72,000
Drawings	32,300	
Inventory at 30 September 2011	16,449	
Non-current assets at cost		
cost	85,000	
provision for depreciation at 30 September 2011		47,800
Prepayments	1,042	
Profit for year		
Trade payables		14,113
Trade receivables	18,203	
Suspense account	1,098	
	154,092	154,092

Krisha reports that several errors have been made in the accounting records. These are as follows:

1 An error was made in calculating the inventory at 30 September 2011. Items valued at cost £420 had been overlooked.

2 The annual depreciation had been calculated as 20% on cost. However, the business's policy is to charge depreciation at 15% on cost.

3 Owner's drawings of £560 had not been posted from the cash book.

4 Discounts allowed of £269 had been added to the gross profit rather than deducted.

(a) Calculate a revised profit for the year ended 30 September 2011 correcting the errors listed above.

(b) Prepare a statement of financial position (balance sheet) at 30 September 2011.

4   Anita Chan has produced the following statement of financial position (balance sheet) at the end of her business's accounting year. The statement of financial position (balance sheet) contains errors.

Statement of financial position (balance sheet) at 31 January 2011			
	£	£	£
NON-CURRENT (FIXED) ASSETS			240,000
CURRENT ASSETS			
Inventory	32,000		
Trade receivables	7,420		
Prepayments	617		
Cash at bank	594		
		40,631	
less CURRENT LIABILITIES			
Trade payables	11,390		
Accruals	1,235		
		12,625	
			28,006
			268,006
less NON-CURRENT LIABILITIES			
Bank loan			14,000
			254,006
CAPITAL			
Opening balance		240,016	
Profit (net profit)		47,448	
		287,464	
Drawings		33,458	
			254,006

Anita reports that the following errors have been discovered.

1   A payment to a trade payable of £885 on 31 January had not been recorded in the books of account.

2   The account of a trade receivable with a balance of £228 should have been written off as a bad debt.

3   When preparing the income statement an accrual of £118 had been overlooked.

4   The inventory on 31 January 2011 was overstated by £600.

Prepare a revised statement of financial position (balance sheet) taking account of the errors listed above.

Financial and management accounting

Chapters in this unit:

Introduction to Unit 2

As you start this new unit you should feel you have developed skills in preparing double entry accounting records for a sole trader. You should also feel competent in preparing income statements and statements of financial position (balance sheets). All the work you have done to date will now be valuable as you focus your attention on this new unit, in which you are going to develop much more skill in preparing financial statements, and broaden your understanding of accounting principles and of the main types of business ownership.

In **Chapter 5** you are going to look at the three main types of business organisation: sole traders, partnership and limited liability companies. You are going to find out why each of these types would be appropriate for particular circumstances.

In **Chapter 6** you are going to develop an understanding of the fundamental rules that all accountants use when preparing accounting records. These fundamental rules are normally referred to as 'accounting concepts'. You will find that you have been applying many of these rules already without realising it.

Chapter 7 provides an opportunity for you to develop your skills in preparing financial statements. You will be able to use your knowledge of making adjustments applying these procedures to income such as rent receivable. You will learn how to ensure that a business's profit is calculated as realistically as possible by ensuring that some account is taken of the likelihood of there being bad debts. You will also extend your knowledge of depreciation. This chapter will also help you make sure you can distinguish correctly between amounts spent on everyday running costs and money spent on non-current assets, that is correctly identify revenue and capital expenditure.

In **Chapter 8** you will apply your understanding of the financial statements to limited liability companies. As well as preparing company financial statements you will learn about much of the terminology that is commonly associated with limited companies. You will also learn some advanced techniques that are used to revalue non-current assets, issue shares to existing shareholders ('rights issues') and restructure a company's statement of financial position (balance sheet) by making what is often called a bonus issue of shares.

In **Chapter 9** you will learn how to make use of financial accounting information and how to provide the owner of a business, the manager of the business, or other interested parties, with data about how the business is performing. This important process is achieved by using accounting ratios and by interpreting the results of ratio calculations.

You will learn how to write effective reports on business performance that provide a reliable evaluation of performance and include recommendations on how to make further progress. In other words you will be helping the owner(s) of businesses to manage their business more effectively.

Chapter 10 introduces the idea of preparing information about the future of a business instead of looking back to what has already happened. The chapter is concerned with budgets. You will learn why budgets are a potentially valuable tool for business owners and managers, but also why budgets, if not used properly, can cause problems for businesses. You will also learn how to prepare a cash budget.

In the final chapter – **Chapter 11** – you will have the opportunity to consider why almost all businesses rely on computers and computer software to produce their financial records. You will learn about the overwhelming advantages of computerisation, but also consider the potential disadvantages of relying on computers and software programmes to produce accounting information.

When you are assessed on this unit you can expect to be asked to prepare the financial statements of sole traders as well as limited companies. Questions could range from those requiring a short response, requiring just a small section of a business's financial statement, to those requiring a much more extensive answer encompassing most if not all of these financial statements. In addition, questions requiring a computational response could require ledger accounts in which you demonstrate your understanding of a variety of topics, for example provisions for depreciation, provisions for doubtful debts, etc. You might also, of course, be asked to calculate ratios or prepare a cash budget.

Do not forget that you will also be asked to write about accounting topics as well. Expect to have to respond to questions requiring explanations of accounting concepts or techniques. There could be questions requiring a more lengthy response, perhaps a report in which you set out an evaluation or discussion about a particular topic, for example a business's performance or the arguments for and against forms of ownership or computerising accounting records.

5   Types of business organisation

In this chapter you will learn:

- that there are three different types of ownership: sole trader, partnership and limited liability company

- how to explain the advantages that arise from each of the three types of ownership

- how to explain the disadvantages that arise from each of the three types of ownership.

Links

- Partnerships are covered in more detail in *A2 Accounting*, Unit 3.

- Limited companies are covered in more detail in Chapter 8.

Key terms

Sole trader: a business owned by one individual. The individual bears sole responsibility for the business's actions.

Unlimited liability: the owner of a business is fully responsible for all the debts of the business.

This chapter compares three important types of business organisation. You will be able to gain an understanding of the broad range of factors that need to be considered before deciding which type of organisation is the most appropriate depending on circumstances. You will find that you are already very familiar with sole traders from the subject matter you have already covered. For example, from preparing double entry accounts and financial statements, you will know that a sole trader provides all the capital in this type of business, and is rewarded by having access to any profits in the form of drawings. You will also be aware that a sole trader has to take full responsibility for the business's activities. However, this chapter is likely to introduce you to partnerships and to limited companies for the first time.

Sole traders

What are the advantages of being a sole trader?

The **sole trader** is the only person responsible for the business and so decision making is potentially faster. Owners of this type of organisation often say that they enjoy the feeling of independence and being in control. Furthermore, sole-trader businesses are usually reasonably straightforward to establish because there are (normally) relatively few bureaucratic requirements. Of course, all the profits made by the business belong to the sole trader and these can be withdrawn in the form of cash drawings.

What are the disadvantages?

Sole traders have **unlimited liability** for the debts of their business, so if the business fails they could lose both the business's assets and also their private possessions.

The amount of capital that can be invested is likely to be limited to the wealth of one individual and this could restrict the size of the business.

Sole traders often find owning a business a great tie; some sole traders work long hours, have few holidays and sometimes rather poor rewards. They can sometimes feel they operate in isolation and do not have the support or access to the expertise available in other forms of ownership.

On the death of the sole trader the business would cease to operate.

Case study

Sally Amis becomes a sole trader

Sally Amis started her business in 1995 offering home owners advice on interior design. She had studied interior design at college

Consider the case of Sally Amis as described in the case study.

1 Summarise in a few words two main advantages of Sally being a sole trader.

2 Summarise in a few words two main disadvantages of Sally being a sole trader.

Key terms

Partnership: where two or more individuals run a continuing business for profit.

Background knowledge

Partnerships occur where a number of individuals join together in business with a view to making a profit. Partners normally make formal agreements about profit sharing and prepare what is a called a 'deed of partnership'.

AQA Examiner's tip

You are only expected to have an understanding of the advantages and disadvantages of being in partnership for this unit.

Link

Accounting for partnerships is studied in detail in A2 *Accounting*, Unit 3.

and with limited private resources she found it relatively easy to start her business. She visited her customers' homes offering advice on soft furnishings and décor. She gained a lot of satisfaction from being in charge of her own affairs, but she worked very long hours and, without anyone else to discuss ideas with, found she did make a number of mistakes, some of them rather costly. It took a number of years to build up the business's reputation and a strong customer base, and profits were relatively low to start with.

Partnerships

What are the advantages of being in partnership?

Partners have access to more finance than a sole trader because there are more individuals who can make capital contributions.

Partnerships are quite often formed so that the particular expertise or specialised skills and knowledge of individuals can be guaranteed to be available. In addition, partners can often share the management responsibilities of a business, making the workload more manageable and making it possible to share ideas.

What are the disadvantages?

Partnerships, like sole traders, have unlimited liability for the debts of the business. Moreover, partners have to share whatever profits or losses are made by the business.

Decision making can be more difficult because it will be necessary to obtain the agreement of all the partners to important aspects of running the business. Sometimes good ideas may have to be abandoned because one or more partners will not agree to their implementation.

Partnerships can be relatively short-lived because they may close on the death or retirement of a partner.

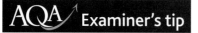

Case study

Sally forms a partnership with Riccardo Verdi

Sally Amis's interior design business was doing quite well by 2003. Sally was aware, however, that in order to expand she would need more finance, and she was also aware that she needed to gain more expertise in order to offer advice about the latest developments in paints and emulsions. Since 2001 she had occasionally worked with a friend of hers, Riccardo Verdi, who had not only the private resources but also the expertise she needed. Early in 2004, Sally and Riccardo formed a partnership. Immediately the new firm of Amis and Verdi was able to offer a much fuller service to many more customers. Profits were higher than for Sally's business as a sole trader. However, these profits now had to be shared between Sally and Riccardo. Sally noticed that she was less likely to make mistakes simply because she could talk things through with Riccardo. As a result they were both able to offer better advice to customers. Sally and Riccardo generally got on very well together, but there were times when they found it difficult to reach agreement on some important decisions.

Activities

Consider the case of Sally Amis and Riccardo Verdi as they form their partnership.

1 Summarise in a few words two main advantages of Sally and Riccardo being a partnership.

2 Summarise in a few words two main disadvantages of Sally and Riccardo being a partnership.

Limited liability companies

What are the advantages of forming a limited liability company?

■ Shareholders in a **limited liability company** enjoy the protection of **'limited liability'** which means that if the company fails they can lose the amount they have invested (or promised to invest) but no more. Unlike a sole trader or partner they do not risk losing their private possessions.

■ Limited companies can raise large amounts of finance. There is the potential to have many shareholders investing in a company. Because companies have a separate legal identify to that of their owners, they can continue to operate irrespective of changes in ownership.

■ There is the possibility of sharing ideas and management of the business with a wider group of individuals.

What are the disadvantages?

■ Limited liability companies are subject to many legal requirements. For example, it is more difficult to form a limited company and, once established, directors are required to send a copy of the company's annual accounts to the Registrar of Companies; except in the case of the smallest companies, their accounts must be audited.

■ From the point of view of those who first establish a limited company, there is the possibility that the control of the company could change over time as individual shareholders acquire or sell shares. This is because shares normally carry voting rights that can be used at shareholders' meetings, and so whoever owns more than 50% of the shares with voting rights, effectively controls the company.

Case study

Sally and Riccardo establish a limited company

Sally and Riccardo's partnership prospered. By 2008 they found that demand for their interior design advice was so great that they often had to turn customers away. They both felt that there was a real opportunity to expand their business still further, but that this would require far more capital. They were also very conscious that if things went wrong, they could lose all the money they had invested in the partnership and their private possessions as well. They decided the best way forward was to form a private limited company, Amis Verdi Ltd. Sally and Riccardo owned the majority of the shares in the company and they became the company's directors with responsibility for the day-to-day management of the business. Some of their key staff also became shareholders. All the shareholders clearly understood that the maximum they could lose was the amount they invested in the company's shares. The

Key terms

Limited liability company: a form of organisation whose owners (or members) own shares and where the owners enjoy the benefit of having limited liability for the debts of the business. Companies have a separate existence from their owners.

Limited liability: the responsibility of the owners of the business (shareholders) for the debts of the business is limited to the amount they have agreed to invest.

Background knowledge

There are two principle types of limited company. A private limited company (Ltd) must have one or more members (shareholders) but its shares are not available to the general public. A public limited company (plc) must have at least two shareholders and can offer shares to the public. A public limited company must have have issued shares to the value of at least £50,000 before it can trade.

Link

Limited liability companies and the preparation of their financial statements are covered in more detail in Chapter 8. See page 112 for more background information about limited liability companies.

company's founders soon realised that they had to comply with many regulations when setting up the company. For example, the company had to be registered at Companies House and this meant sending several documents and completing complicated forms.

AQA Examiner's tip

Remember in an evaluation question like Question 3, you are expected to present a balanced argument and to come to a clear recommendation.

Activities

Consider the case of Sally and Riccardo as they convert their partnership into a private limited liability company.

1 Summarise in a few words two main advantages that will be enjoyed by Sally and Riccardo as the major shareholders in Amis Verdi Ltd.

2 Summarise in a few words two main disadvantages that may be arise from forming a private limited liability company.

Learning outcomes

As a result of studying this chapter, you should now be able to:

- define the terms sole trader, partnership, limited liability company, limited liability and unlimited liability
- explain the advantages and disadvantages of being a sole trader and being in a partnership
- explain the advantages and disadvantages of forming a limited liability company
- compare and evaluate the different types of ownership
- prepare a statement or report advising an individual or individuals whether or not to adopt a particular form of ownership

AQA Examination Style Questions

1 From the point of view of sharing profits and losses, contrast the three forms of business ownership: sole trader; partnership and limited liability company.

2 Adrian Webster has been in business as a sole trader for a number of years. He feels that the time is now right to expand his business. He has been considering entering partnership or forming a private limited company. He is clear of the relative merits of these two forms of ownership, but is not sure what the potential disadvantages might be. Explain the disadvantages of forming (i) a partnership, and (ii) a private limited company to Adrian.

3 Carmen Garcia is the owner of a very successful garden landscaping business. She has decided to form a private limited company in which she will be the sole shareholder. Evaluate Carmen's decision and explain the significance of her being the only shareholder.

6 Accounting concepts

All the accounting procedures and techniques that you are learning as part of your A Level course follow a set of basic rules that have been carefully developed by the accountancy profession. Knowledge of these rules will enable you gain a better understanding of some new techniques and procedures that you will be learning in this and subsequent units. You will find that you have already been applying these rules without realising it, in much of the subject matter you have covered so far. For example, you will remember how, in Unit 1, you learned the technique for adjusting expenses for prepayments or amounts due when preparing an income statement. This technique is based on a basic accounting rule called the 'accruals concept' that is covered in this chapter. As a second example, you will be quite used by now to recording the removal of the business's cash by the owner for private use in a separate drawings account. This transaction is recorded in this way as a result of the 'entity concept', which is also explained more fully in this chapter. Accounting concepts affect virtually every aspect of financial accounting and you will find that they are often referred to as you proceed through the remainder of this unit and through the main elements of the A2 accounting course.

Purpose of accounting concepts

What is the point of accounting concepts?

Accounting concepts are the fundamental rules that are to be followed by all those preparing accounting records. These rules ensure that everyone treats particular situations in the same way. An understanding of the concepts is vital for anyone preparing accounting records because they provide guidelines for the treatment of new or unfamiliar accounting problems. As a result, those using accounting statements can be confident in the information, because they can feel assured that the content would have been very much the same whichever accountant had prepared the statements.

You will find that many of the concepts seem like common sense. This is partly because you have unconsciously been applying them already.

Objectivity

Wherever possible, accounting information should be factual (that is objective) rather than someone's opinion (that is subjective). Accountants prefer facts, rather than opinion, because normally facts can be more easily agreed, where someone's opinion is likely to be disputed.

The **objectivity** concept is at the heart of any rules about valuing assets (see the cost concept).

Note: in some situations, of course, opinion cannot be avoided. The depreciation charge on a non-current asset depends on estimates of economic life, possible residual value, and the method of depreciation to be used.

AQA Examiner's tip

You would not be alone if you found these concepts quite difficult to grasp initially. It may help to spread out this topic over a period of time (perhaps a few days, or even a few weeks) doing a little at a time, and gradually building up an understanding.

Key terms

Objectivity: factual information is preferred because it is likely to be beyond dispute.

Cost

Assets should be valued at **cost**. This is because this is an objective valuation (see objectivity) rather than a matter of opinion.

■ Case study

Sally Thomas applies the cost and objectivity concepts

Sally Thomas, who owns a business called Thomas & Co, has been told that some office equipment, which originally cost £12,000 and on which depreciation of £8,000 has been charged, would now cost £14,500 to replace. Sally wonders whether the equipment's value should be adjusted to take account of the increasing cost of replacement. Sally is advised by the business's accountant to ignore the replacement value of the equipment. The accountant has said that it is uncertain just how much it would cost to replace these assets, because it would depend on many factors including which supplier was used. In other words, £14,500 as a value is a matter of opinion (subjective), whereas the original cost of £12,000 can be established by the evidence in the form of invoices for the equipment (objective). The business should continue to value the office equipment objectively using cost.

■ Background knowledge

The rule is sometimes called the 'historic cost' concept.

■ Key terms

Going concern: the assumption that a business will continue to trade for the foreseeable future.

Going concern

Those preparing financial statements are to assume that the business will continue to trade for the foreseeable future (at least one year). As a result the possible resale value of assets can definitely be ignored, because the assumption is that the assets are not for sale. In other words, the **going concern** concept supports the idea of using cost as the basis of valuing assets.

Note: the going concern concept would have to be set aside, however, if it was known that a business, or part of a business, is likely to close in the near future.

■ Case study

Greg Hardy applies the going concern concept

Greg Hardy, who owns a business called Hardy Cycles, has been told that some office furniture that cost £12,000 and on which depreciation £8,000 has been written off, is likely to have a resale value of only £500. Greg wonders whether the furniture should be reduced in value in the business's books. Greg is advised by the business's accountant to ignore the possible resale value of the furniture because the business is going to continue to trade and it will make use of the office furniture for the foreseeable future.

■ Activity

Harry Roberts is the owner of a business that includes a motor vehicle among its non-current assets. Harry is able to supply the following information about this vehicle:

- the motor vehicle cost £25,000 when it was purchased several years ago
- a similar model would now cost £28,000 to buy
- if the vehicle was offered for sale a local dealer would be prepared to offer £21,000 for it.

Referring to as many relevant accounting concepts as possible, explain how you would value this motor vehicle in the business's books of account. Comment on whether there are any circumstances when you think it might be appropriate to use the local dealer's valuation of £21,000.

Accruals

Profits should be calculated for a period of time, ensuring that revenue for that period is matched with the expenses incurred in earning that revenue.

The **accruals** concept is the fundamental rule about how profits should be calculated. It means that profits are based on revenue and expenses for a time period, whether or not money has been received or paid. It is the reason for many of the special features of financial statements, such as making adjustments for unsold inventory and for expenses due or prepaid.

Illustration

How to apply the accruals concept

Closing inventory: when preparing an income statement it is important to deduct closing inventory from the cost of sales. Although this inventory will have been paid for during that period, it is really a cost for next period when the goods are sold.

Depreciation: when preparing an income statement it is important to include an estimate of contribution made by each non-current asset to earning the business's revenue (in end of year financial statements) for that period, even though the payment for the non-current asset will probably have been made several years before.

Expense adjustments: the amount of an expense for a trading period is quite often out of step with the amount actually paid. As a result it is necessary to take account of amounts due but unpaid (accruals), or amounts paid in advance (prepayments) when preparing financial statements.

Activity

Laura Kemp is preparing her business's financial statements. She has been advised that she should take account of the following matters:

a an expense has been prepaid

b rent receivable is due but not yet received

c there is a closing inventory of unsold goods

d annual depreciation of the business's fixtures and fittings.

In each case explain to Laura in what way she will be applying the accruals concept when taking account of these matters.

Consistency

The **consistency** concept requires businesses to apply the same accounting procedures and policies from one financial period to the next. This ensures that financial statements are prepared in the same way each year. As a result, the users of the financial statements can feel confident that comparisons they make will have some validity.

Case study

Asha Chibuzo applies the consistency concept

Asha Chibuzo owns a business that uses the straight-line method of depreciation. She has been told that this method should be used each year. There should not be a sudden switch to the reducing-balance method of depreciation. Such a change would have a distorting effect on the reported profit for that business for the year in which the change was made, compared to the previous year.

Asha has also been told that if overriding reasons can be found for changing accounting procedures and policies, the consistency rule can be ignored. However, the accounting statements affected by the change should clearly show the effect of the change. Users of the accounts can then make a suitable adjustment when comparing results from one year to the next.

Activity

An individual is looking at the financial results of a limited company for each of the last 3 years. How does that individual benefit from the fact that the limited company's accountant will have applied the consistency concept?

Key terms

Consistency: accounting methods are applied in the same way in each accounting period.

Prudence: where there is doubt, asset and profit values are under- rather than overstated, never assume profit until realised, but losses should be dealt with when anticipated.

Materiality: if the amount involved is relatively insignificant, then the usual accounting treatment of an item can be set aside.

Background knowledge

The prudence concept is sometimes referred to as 'conservatism'.

Prudence

Where there is doubt, asset values and profits should be understated rather than overstated. This rule, called the **prudence** concept, ensures that those who have a stake in a business are not misled into thinking that the business is doing better than it really is.

Case study

Hershel applies the prudence concept

Hershel is the owner of a retail business. Hershel's business sold some goods on credit. The amount due has been outstanding from the receivable for some time. All attempts to contact the customer have failed. Hershel has been prudent and written off the bad debt in the accounts, rather than give an unduly optimistic view of the receivables and profits for the year on the business's statement of financial position (balance sheet).

Materiality

The **materiality** concept concerns the treatment of certain items when preparing financial statements. The rule requires that care should be taken to ensure that all information provided is significant to the users of the statements, i.e. it should matter. In other words, trivial items should not be included.

Case study

Ingrid Magna applies the materiality concept

Ingrid Magna owns a travel agency specialising in winter sports holidays. Ingrid purchased a new paper shredder for use in the office at cost of £80. Ingrid was advised not to record this as a non-current asset, nor subject the item to an annual depreciation charge, on the grounds that it simply would not be worth all the effort to do so. Instead, this minor item of office equipment was written off in that year's income statement.

Realisation

At the heart of the **realisation** concept is the idea that revenue should be recognised when it is certain. In other words a sale should only be included in a business's profit calculations for a financial period if cash has already been paid or there is a promise to pay cash. In practice, a sale is regarded as certain when cash has been paid or an invoice has been issued.

Case study

Lydia French applies the realisation concept

On the last day of the financial year Lydia French notes that her business has cash sales of £8,000, that she has issued invoices to customers totalling £5,000 and that the business has received orders from regular customers totalling £3,000. Lydia records the day's sales as £13,000. Lydia ignores the orders because there is no certainty that they will become definite sales. Lydia might not, for example, be able to fulfil the orders, or the customer might cancel the order.

Business entity

The idea behind the **business entity** concept is that transactions recorded in an organisation's accounts can only relate to that organisation. In other words, transactions relating to the owner's private affairs cannot be recorded in the accounts of the organisation.

Case study

Steve Merritt applies the business entity concept

Steve Merritt is a sole trader. Recently, he used his own resources to pay for a holiday for his family. Steve did not make any record of this transaction in the business's books of account because the transaction did not affect the business.

If Steve had used the business's cash to pay for the holiday, it would be necessary to record the transaction in the business's cash book and drawings account; it would, of course, be incorrect to debit the business's travel expenses account.

Activity

Find out about the policy for writing off low-value non-current assets in the organisation in which you are currently learning/working. In addition, find out about some recent examples of the policy being applied to some low cost items that would otherwise have been regarded as non-current assets.

Background knowledge

Organisations devise their own policy about what should count as material and what value should be regarded as too low in value to warrant recording as a non-current asset. For example, a small organisation might regard expenditure on an asset costing below £500 as an amount to be written off immediately.

Key terms

Realisation: revenue should not be recorded in the accounts until it is realised, i.e. when there is cash or the promise of cash.

Business entity: an accounting system will contain records of that organisation only.

Activity

June Blakey is a sole trader. During the most recently completed financial year the following transactions occurred affecting June and/or her business:

a June took inventory from the business's storerooms for her private use, value £400

b June paid her business's electricity bill, £350, from her private resources

c June paid for some kitchen fittings for her family home and paid for these from her personal bank account.

Applying the entity concept, in each case state the double entry, if any, required in the business's books of account to record these transactions.

Applying concepts to the valuation of inventory

Inventory valuation provides a good example of how concepts are applied. In particular two concepts feature in an important rule about inventory valuation: cost and prudence.

Inventory, like any asset, should be valued at cost.

However, the prudence concept states that where there is doubt, asset values should be under- rather than overstated.

Bearing these points in mind consider the following illustrations.

Illustration

How to apply the rule about inventory valuation

Denise notes that her business has an inventory of 20 items in stock that cost £30 each; these items would normally have a selling price of £40 each. Two items are damaged. Denise believes they could be sold at £33 each, but £5 will need to be spent on each of the damaged items in order to put them in a fit state for sale.

Step 1 18 items can be valued at cost £30, total £540

Step 2 Looking carefully at the 2 damaged items the following facts emerge:

- each cost £30
- each could be sold for £33, but in each case the sale at £33 will only take place having spent a further £5, giving a net sale value of £28 per item.

Following the prudence concept, the 2 items should be valued at £28 each (i.e. the net resale value) because it is lower than cost. In other words, where there is doubt, we have under- rather than overvalued items.

The inventory will be worth £540 + (2 × £28) i.e. £596.

Some new terms can be used in connection with valuing inventories:

Realisable value – simply means the sale value that can actually be achieved

Net realisable value – means sale value but taking account of any costs that must be incurred before the sale can take place

Key terms

Realisable value: sale value.

Net realisable value: sale value less any costs necessary to incur a sale.

Summary:

The rule that is applied to valuing inventory is as follows:

'inventories must be valued at cost or net realisable value, whichever is lower'.

Learning outcomes

As a result of studying this chapter, you should now be able to:

- explain the purpose of accounting concepts
- define each of the nine accounting concepts, explain their purpose and give examples of their use.
- explain how accounting concepts are applied to inventory valuation
- define terms used in connection with inventory valuation such as net realisable value
- calculate inventory values based on the application of accounting concepts

Activity

Nimesh, the owner of a retail business, discovered that an inventory of 20 items that had cost £30 each have been slightly damaged. These items would normally have a selling price of £40 each. However, Nimesh expects that having repackaged each of these items at a cost of £4 each, they can be sold for £31 each. Calculate the total value of these 20 items for inclusion in the business's closing inventory.

AQA Examination Style Questions

1   Identify the concept(s) being applied in each of the following.

Transaction	Concept(s)
When preparing the income statement an adjustment was to an expense account for an accrual	
The owner of a business paid for a gift for a member of the family using the business's money. This transaction was debited to the drawings account	
A bad debt was written off promptly.	(1)
	(2)
A business has used the straight-line method of depreciation every year.	(1)
	(2)

2   When preparing a business's final accounts the closing inventory included 185 items which had cost £36 each and which are normally sold for £54 each. However, it appears that 16 of these items are damaged and that in the case of all of the damaged items the selling price will have to be reduced by £15 each. Furthermore, in the case of 8 of the damaged items some minor repairs will be required prior to sale costing £7 per item.

   (a)   Explain the rule for valuing inventories, referring to appropriate accounting concepts.

   (b)   Calculate the value of the 185 items to be recorded in the business's financial statements.

3   Explain why the correct application of accounting concepts is important to the users of accounting statements.

7

Financial statements of sole traders

In this chapter you will be able to develop your skills in preparing the end-of-year financial statements of sole traders. You will be able to build on the techniques you learnt in Unit 1 where you prepared basic income statements and statements of financial position (balance sheets). You will find that your understanding of how expense items are adjusted for prepayments and amounts due can now be applied to income items. You will develop your knowledge of depreciation and learn how it is recorded in ledger accounts as well as in the financial statements. This chapter will introduce you to some more sophisticated techniques that are designed to ensure that the important task of calculating profits is carried out in a systematic and fair way to properly reflect a business's performance. You will learn how to reduce a business's profits based on an estimate of amounts that will be lost in future because some receivables are unlikely to pay. You will also learn how to distinguish between two types of expenditure (revenue and capital) that will be important if you are to produce accurate profit calculations. All these new techniques will also be of value when you prepare the end-of-year financial statements of other organisations such as limited companies.

Link

- You will study limited companies in Chapter 8
- You will study partnerships in *A2 Accounting*, Unit 3

---

1 Bad debts recovered and income received in advance and due

In this topic you will learn:

- how to explain the term 'bad debts recovered'
- how to explain potential sources of income for a sole trader
- how to record bad debts recovered in ledger accounts and in financial statements
- how to record adjustments to income when preparing financial statements

Bad debts recovered

What is a bad debt recovered?

When a receivable cannot pay the amount due because of bankruptcy, the account is written off as a bad debt. However, sometimes a receivable will pay the amount due after a business has written off the receivable's account as a bad debt. The amount is recorded as a '**bad debt recovered**'. The recovery of a bad debt is, of course, good news for a business.

How is a bad debt recovered recorded?

Step 1: Reinstate the receivable's account:

Dr Receivable

Cr Bad Debts Recovered

Step 2: Record the amount received from the receivable

Dr Bank Account

Cr Receivable

The balance of a bad debt recovered account is subsequently transferred to the profit and loss section of the income statement at the business's year end. The amount will be **recorded as a gain** in the **income statement**.

Case study

Murray Traders

Jim Murray is the owner of a wholesale business called Murray Traders. The business sells clothes and footwear for the young adult market. As a wholesaler the business has many credit customers ranging from small retail shops to some of the larger well-known chains. The business owns extensive freehold premises part of which has been sublet to a tenant. In recent years, Jim Murray has invested the business's surplus cash in a number of investments.

Illustration

How to record a bad debts recovered in the ledger accounts

On 12 February 2010 a business, Murray Traders, received a cheque from Tom Scott for £1,840. Tom Scott had owed the business this sum, but his account had been written off as a bad debt six months previously.

Record this information is the business's books of account. Show how this information would be recorded in the business's trial balance, bad debts recovered account, and income statement.

> **Link**
>
> For more information on bad debts, see Chapter 4, page 64.

> **Key terms**
>
> **Bad debt recovered:** an amount received from a receivable that has previously been written off.
>
> **Income received in advance:** money received by a business as income but that relates to the next financial period.

Dr	Receivable: Tom Scott				Cr
Feb 12	Bad debts recovered	580	Feb 12	Bank	580

Dr	Cash Book (extract)				Cr
		Cash	Bank	Cash	Bank
Feb 12	Receivable: Tom Scott		580		

Dr	Bad Debts Recovered Account				Cr
Dec 31	Income statement	1,840	Feb 12	Tom Scott	1,840

Trial Balance (extract) at 31 December 2010		
	Dr	Cr
	£	£
Bad debts recovered		1,840

> **Activity**
>
> Jim Murray, the owner of 'Murray Traders' has just received a cheque from another receivable, Sarah Cameron, for £320. Sarah's account had been written off several years ago as a bad debt. Explain to Jim Murray how this bad debt recovered should be treated when preparing an income statement?

Income Statement (Extract)
for the year ended 31 December 2010

		£	£
Gross Profit			184,500
Add	**Bad debt recovered**		**1,840**
			186,340
Less	Business rates	11,450	
	Insurance etc.	3,720	

Figure 7.1 *How to record a bad debts recovered*

Income received in advance

What is income received in advance?

Taking rent receivable as an example of income received in advance, it is possible for a tenant to pay rent in advance. If the rent is received for a period stretching into the next financial year, it will be necessary to adjust the amount to be recorded in the profit and loss section of the income statement, so that it records rent receivable only for this financial year.

Rent receivable which has been received in advance is a **current liability**.

Illustration

How to record income received in advance

Murray Traders sublets part of its premises. The business had received a total of £3900 from its tenant for rent during the year ended 31 December 2011. This amount includes a payment for one month's rent of £300 for January 2012.

How would this information be recorded in the business's rent receivable account? Show how rent receivable will appear in the trial balance, income statement for the year ended 31 December 2011 and statement of financial position (balance sheet) at 31 December 2011.

Step 1: record the receipt of £3,900 in the rent receivable account

Step 2: transfer the appropriate amount to the income statement

Step 3: balance the account

Dr			Rent Receivable Account				Cr
Dec	31	Income statement	3600	Dec	31	Total receipts	3,900
	31	Balance c/d	300				
			3900				3,900
				Jan	1	Balance b/d	300

Trial balance entry

Trial Balance (Extract) at
31 December 2011

	Dr	Cr
	£	£
Rent receivable		3,900

Income statement entry

Income Statement (Extract)
for the year ended 31 December 2011

	£	£
Gross Profit		83,780
Add: rent receivable		
(£3900 – £300)		<u>3,600</u>
		87,380
Less: advertising	4,500	
bank charges	670	
etc.		

Statement of financial position (balance sheet) entry

Statement of financial position (balance sheet) (Extract) at 31 December 2011

Current liabilities	£
Rent received in advance	300

Figure 7.2 *Recording income received in advance*

Income due

What is income due?

Taking interest receivable as an example of **income due**, frequently the dates when interest is received by a business will not match the business's financial period. It is possible, therefore, that at the end of a financial year interest may still be due on savings or an investment, but will not actually be received until the next financial period.

Illustration

How to record income due

Murray Traders has received £4,800 in interest on an investment account during the year ended 31 December 2011. At 31 December 2011 interest £420 is due but not yet received.

How should this information be recorded in the Interest Received Account? Show how interest received should be recorded in the trial balance for the year ended 31 December 2011 and statement of financial position (balance sheet) at 31 December 2011.

Dr		**Interest Received Account**					Cr
Dec	31	Income statement	5,240	Dec	31	Total receipts	4,800
					31	Balance c/d	420
			5,240				5,240
Jan	1	Balance b/d	420				

Step 1: Record the receipt of £4,800 in the interest received account

Step 2: Transfer the appropriate amount to the income statement

Step 3: Balance the account

Trial balance entry

Trial Balance (Extract) at 31 December 2011

	Dr	Cr
	£	£
Interest received		4,800

Income statement entry

Income statement (Extract)
for the year ended 31 December 2011

	£	£
Gross Profit		154,000
Add: interest received **(£4800+£420)**		**5,240**
		159,240
Less: business rates	9,200	
carriage outwards etc	3,220	

Statement of financial position (balance sheet) at
31 December 2011 (Extract)

Current assets	£
Interest received due	420

Figure 7.3 *Recording income due*

Background knowledge

Making adjustments in income accounts is another example of the application of the accruals concept.

Activity

Explain to Jim Murray why income due is shown as a current asset on a statement of financial position (balance sheet).

AQA Examiner's tip

It is important to show workings when answering examination questions. So if you have to adjust income, show details of how you reached the figure to be shown in the income statement.

Learning outcomes

As a result of studying this topic, you should now be able to:

- define bad debts recovered, income received in advance and income due
- record these items in ledger accounts
- prepare financial statements of a sole trader that include bad debts recovered and adjustments for income received in advance and due
- record income received and advance and income due on a statement of financial position

AQA Examination Style Questions

1   The end of year income statement for Samson Estates & Co includes income from three different sources. The following details are available about income for the year ended 31 December 2011.

	Amount received during year ended 31 December 2011	Additional information at 31 December 2011	Amount to be transferred to income statement for year ended 31 December 2011	Entry on statement of financial position at 31 December 2011 (select the correct answer)
Commission received	£13,550	Commission of £830 is due but not yet received	£.............	Current asset £830 or current liability £830?
Interest received	£3,840	Interest of £180 related to the year ending 31 December 2012	£.............	Current asset £180 or current liability £180?
Rent received	£83,800	A tenant has paid rent of £720 in advance for 2012; another tenant owes rent of £950 for December 2011	£.............	Current asset £720 or current asset £950; or current liability £720 or current liability of £950?

2   'Platinum Software' is a wholesale business owned by Rajiv. The trading section of the business's income statement has already been completed. The business's trial balance at 31 August 2011 was as follows:

	Dr £000	Cr £000
Bad debts	14	
Bad debts recovered		6
Bank overdraft		5
Capital		452
Commission receivable		33
Drawings	62	
Gross profit		884
Inventory at 31 August 2011	53	
Non-current		
cost	1,400	
provision for depreciation at 1 September 2010		364
Operating expenses	227	
Rent receivable		14
Trade payables		24
Trade receivables	26	
	1782	1782

Additional information at 31 August 2011 (all figures in thousands)
- Operating expenses due but unpaid, £6
- Depreciation on non-current assets totals £48
- Rent receivable of £15 has been received in advance
- Commission receivable of £11 is due but not yet received

Prepare an income statement for the year ended 31 August 2011 and a statement of financial position (balance sheet) at that date. Show how the rent receivable account should appear in the business's general ledger balanced at 31 August 2011.

3   Cheryl Manning owns a retail store. The following trial balance was extracted from the business's books at the end of its most recently completed financial year, 28 February 2012.

	Dr £	Cr £
Bad debts recovered		1,425
Capital		403,836
Carriage inwards	3,078	
Cash at bank	11,492	
Discounts	557	839
Drawings	41,300	
Freehold premises		
cost	550,000	
provision for depreciation		
at 1 March 2011		99,000
General expenses	8,481	
Interest receivable		332
Investment (current asset)	5,800	
Inventory 1 March 2011	22,715	
Other non-current assets (fixed assets)		
cost	84,600	
provision for depreciation		
at 1 March 2011		33,840
Purchases	375,884	
Rates and insurance	18,556	
Rent receivable		8,360
Returns	4,774	5,883
Revenue		602,471
Trade payables		24,782
Trade receivables	14,831	
Wages	38,700	
	1,180,768	1,180,768

Additional information at 28 February 2012:

- Inventory is £28,455
- Wages due but unpaid £732
- Insurance prepaid £371
- Interest receivable due but not yet received £88
- Rent received in advance £280
- Depreciation should be provided as follows: 2% per annum on the cost of freehold premises; 20% per annum on the cost of other non-current assets.

Prepare an income statement for the year ended 28 February 2012 and a statement of financial position (balance sheet) at that date.

2   Provisions for doubtful debts

Creating a provision for doubtful debts

Why create a provision for doubtful debts?

Businesses have a duty to present a '**true and fair view**' of their affairs. It follows that if a business tends to have bad debts, it should consider reducing the value of its trade receivables when preparing a statement of financial position (balance sheet) to reflect the fact that it is likely that some of the amount shown as due will not be received. This idea of presenting a *fair* view of trade receivables on a statement of financial position (balance sheet) leads to the creation of what is called a **provision for doubtful debts**. A provision for doubtful debts is a good example of the application of the prudence concept.

The amount of the provision for doubtful debts is often based on recent experience of the amount of bad debts in relation to total credit sales.

How to create a provision for doubtful debts

The entries required to create a provision for doubtful debts are:

Debit Income Statement

Credit Provision for Doubtful Debts Account

Illustration

How to create a provision for doubtful debts

Murray Traders has regularly experienced bad debts. On 31 December 2009, the total of trade receivables as shown in the business's sales ledger was £24,000. Based on recent experience, the owner of the business has decided to create a provision for doubtful debts of 5% of trade receivables at the year end.

Record the creation of the provision for doubtful debts in the books of Murray Traders:

Step 1: Calculate the provision: 5% of trade receivables £24,000 = £1,200.

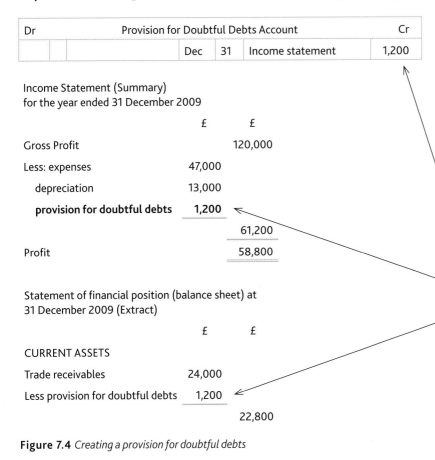

Figure 7.4 *Creating a provision for doubtful debts*

Step 2: Open a provision for doubtful debts account (in the business's general ledger) and make a credit entry for the provision

Step 3: Make a matching debit entry in the income statement

Step 4: Ensure that when trade receivables are recorded on the statement of financial position (balance sheet), they are reduced by the amount of the provision

Activity

Jim Murray has just created a provision for doubtful debts account. However, he says he does not really understand why the account has a credit balance. Explain why a provision for doubtful debts account has a credit balance.

Increasing a provision for doubtful debts

When should a business increase its provision for doubtful debts?

Once a provision for doubtful debts is created it remains in the accounting system, but it is reviewed annually. If there is an increase in the total of trade receivables at the year end, then the provision should be increased to keep in step with this change.

The entries required to increase a provision for doubtful debts are:

Debit Income Statement *with the amount of the increase*

Credit Provision for Doubtful
Debts Account *with the amount of the increase*

Illustration

How to increase a provision for doubtful debts

At 31 December 2010 the total of trade receivables in Murray Traders' sales ledger was £28,000. Jim Murray requires the provision for doubtful debts to be maintained at 5% of trade receivables.

Make entries to maintain the provision for doubtful debts at 5% of trade receivables.

Step 1: Calculate the amount of the revised provision for doubtful debts: 5% × £28,000 = £1,400

Step 2: Calculate the amount by which the existing provision needs to be changed

The existing provision is £1,200 so it will be necessary to add a further £200 to achieve the revised figure of £1,400.

Step 3: Make an entry to alter the existing provision in the provision for doubtful debts account

Step 4: Balance the provision account to show the revised figure for the provision

Dr				Provision for Doubtful Debts Account			Cr
2010				**2009**			
Dec	31	Balance c/d	1,400	Dec	31	Income statement	1,200
				2010			
				Dec	31	Income statement	200
			1,400	**2011**			**1,400**
				Jan	1	Balance b/d	1,400

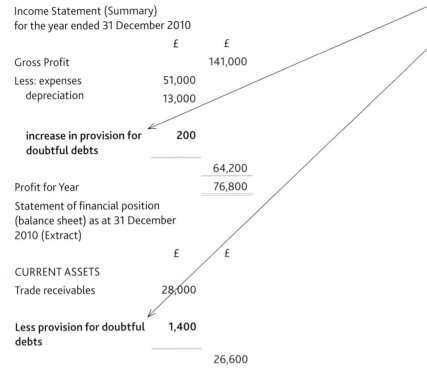

Income Statement (Summary)
for the year ended 31 December 2010

	£	£
Gross Profit		141,000
Less: expenses	51,000	
depreciation	13,000	
increase in provision for doubtful debts	**200**	
		64,200
Profit for Year		76,800

Step 5: Make a matching entry in the income statement

Step 6: Ensure that when the statement of financial position (balance sheet) is prepared the updated balance on the provision for doubtful debts account is deducted from trade debtors

Statement of financial position (balance sheet) as at 31 December 2010 (Extract)

	£	£
CURRENT ASSETS		
Trade receivables	28,000	
Less provision for doubtful debts	**1,400**	
		26,600

Figure 7.5 *Recording an increase in a provision*

Decreasing a provision for doubtful debts

When should a business decrease a provision for doubtful debts?

The total of trade receivables could decrease from one year to the next. In this situation the amount of the provision for doubtful debts should be decreased to keep in step with the decrease in trade receivables.

How should a business decrease its provision for doubtful debts?

The entries required to decrease a provision for doubtful debts are:

Debit Provision for Doubtful
Debts Account   *with the amount of the decrease*

Credit Income Statement   *with the amount of the decrease*

Illustration

How to decrease a provision for doubtful debts

At 31 December 2011 the total of trade receivables in Murray Traders' sales ledger is £22,000. Jim Murray requires the provision for doubtful debts to be maintained at 5% of trade receivables.

Step 1: Calculate the amount of the revised provision for doubtful debts: 5% × £22,00 = £1,100

Step 2: Calculate the amount by which the existing provision needs to be changed

The existing provision is £1,400 so it will be necessary to decrease the provision by £300 to arrive at the revised balance of £1,100.

Dr						Provision for Doubtful Debts Account				Cr
2010					2009				
Dec	31	Balance c/d	1,400		Dec	31	Income statement	1,200
					2010				
					Dec	31	Income statement	200
			1,400					1,400
					2011				
2011					Jan	1	Balance b/d	1,400
Dec	31	Income statement	300					
	31	Balance c/d	1,100					
			1,400		2012			1,400
					Jan	1	Balance b/d	1,100

Step 3: Make an entry to alter the existing provision in the provision for doubtful debts account

Step 4: Balance the provision account to show the revised figure for the provision

Income Statement (Summary) for the year ended 31 December 2011

	£	£
Gross Profit		152,000
Add: decrease in provision for doubtful debts		**300**
		152,300
Less: expenses	57,000	
depreciation	13,000	
		70,000
Profit for Year		82,300

Step 5: Make a matching entry in the income statement

Statement of financial position (balance sheet) as at 31 December 2011 (Extract)

	£	£
CURRENT ASSETS		
Trade receivables	22,000	
Less provision for doubtful debts	1,100	
		20,900

Step 6: Ensure that when the statement of financial position (balance sheet) is prepared the updated balance on the provision for doubtful debts account is deducted from trade receivables

Figure 7.6 *Recording a decrease in a provision*

Learning outcomes

As a result of studying this topic, you should now be able to:

- define the term provision for doubtful debts
- explain why businesses create provisions for doubtful debts
- record provisions for doubtful debts in ledger accounts
- prepare income statements that include the creation of a provision for doubtful debts or an adjustment to an existing provision for doubtful debts
- record a provision for doubtful debts on a statement of financial position (balance sheet)

Examination Style Questions

1   The owner of a business decided that it would be appropriate to introduce a provision for doubtful debts. It was agreed that the provision should be maintained at 5% of trade receivables each year. Trade receivables at the end of each of three recent years were:

Year 1   £28,000

Year 2   £34,000

Year 3   £32,400

Complete the following table recording information about this business's provision for doubtful debts.

Year	Provision for Doubtful Debts £	Amount to be entered in the Income Statement £	Entry in Provision for Doubtful Debts Account (enter Debit or Credit)
1			
2			
3			

2   A business maintains a provision for doubtful debts at 4% of trade receivables at each year end. On 31 December 2009 the balance on the provision account was £880. Trade receivables at 31 December in subsequent years totalled:

2010   £21,200

2011   £23,800

Prepare the provision for doubtful debts account for the three years 2009, 2010 and 2011. Balance the account at the end of 2010 and 2011.

3   Mala owns a retail store. Her business's financial year end is 31 December. The following trial balance was extracted from the business's books of account on 31 December 2011.

	Dr £	Cr £
Bad debts	850	
Bad debts recovered		90
Capital		61,240
Cash at bank	3,890	
Commission received		880
Drawings	31,300	
Equipment		
cost	35,000	
provision for depreciation at 1 January 2011		14,000
Gross profit		151,270
Inventory at 31 December 2011	29,480	
Operating expenses	57,610	
Rent	25,400	
Trade payables		11,850

Trade receivables	27,000	
Vehicles		
cost	45,000	
provision for depreciation at 1 January 2011		16,200
	255,530	255,530

Additional information at 31 December 2011

1   Rent includes a payment of £840 which represents rent for the three months ended 29 February 2012.

2   Operating expenses £740 were due but unpaid.

3   Commission receivable £140 was due but not received at the year end.

4   Tricia decided to create a provision for doubtful debts of 5% of trade receivables at the year end

5   Depreciation was charged on non-current assets as follows:
   - Equipment – 20% per annum using the straight-line method
   - Vehicles – 20% per annum using the straight-line method

Prepare end of year financial statements.

4   Alistair Mackay is the owner of 'Mackay's Bikes'. The business's trial balance on 31 July 2011 was as follows.

	Dr £	Cr £
Bad debts	332	
Bank overdraft		2,765
Business rates	9,074	
Capital		349,188
Carriage outwards	883	
Discounts	1,012	738
Drawings	44,272	
Insurance	3,490	
Inventory at 1 August 2010	33,867	
Light and heat	1,084	
Non-current assets		
cost	740,000	
provision for depreciation at 1 August 2010		321,000
Provision for doubtful debts at 1 August 2010		965
Purchases	404,327	
Rent received		13,850
Revenue		634,881
Trade payables		22,484
Trade receivables	23,200	
Wages and salaries	84,330	
	1,345,871	1,345,871

Additional information at 31 July 2011

1   Inventory was valued at £37,240

2   Prepaid expenses were: administration business rate £285, insurance £430

3   Expenses due but unpaid were: light and heat £244; wages and salaries £884

4   The policy is to maintain the provision for doubtful debts at 5% of trade receivables (debtors) at the year end

5   Depreciation of £51,000 was charged on non-current assets

Prepare the business's income statement for the year ended 31 July 2011 and a statement of financial position (balance sheet) at that date.

3 | Depreciation

AQA Examiner's tip

Try to remember to use some of these technical expressions (such as 'useful economic life') when writing about depreciation.

Key terms

Depreciation: the loss in value of a non-current asset over its useful economic life that is apportioned to financial periods. It is a non-cash expense.

Straight-line method: where the annual depreciation charge is based on the cost of the non-current asset.

Reducing-balance method: where the annual depreciation charge is based on the net book value of the non-current asset at the beginning of each financial period.

Links

The straight-line method can be seen in Chapter 4, pages 63–64.

Understanding and recording depreciation

Why do businesses depreciate non-current assets?

Almost all non-current assets have what is called a useful economic life. This means there is a limited amount of time during which the non-current asset will be of value to a business. The useful life of an asset is limited for a variety of reasons:

- assets lose value as they are used, that is they are subject to wear and tear (example vehicles, buildings)

- some assets are likely to become obsolete due to the pace of technological change; that is cease to be up to date and therefore unable to meet the needs of a business (example office equipment such as computers)

- alternatively, some assets might become inadequate, that is fail to meet the needs of the business because they have limited capacity and the business has grown in size (example, office equipment such as a photocopier)

- some assets' life has a legal limit and becomes valueless at the end of that time (example, the lease of shop premises)

Land is the only obvious exception to the rule that non-current assets should be depreciated. Land is assumed to have an indefinite life.

Depreciation is the means by which the loss in value of a non-current asset is spread out over the useful life of the asset. Depreciation is an expense. It is an example of the application of the accruals concept and ensures that the cost of an asset is matched to the income the asset creates in a financial period.

How is depreciation calculated using the reducing-balance method of depreciation?

As well as the **straight-line method** of depreciation, it is also possible to calculate depreciation basing the annual charge on the net book value of the asset as the beginning of the year, rather than its original cost. This alternative method is called the **reducing-balance method**.

Illustration

How to calculate depreciation using the reducing-balance method

Murray Traders owns a motor vehicle that was purchased on 1 January 2009 for £18,000. It is the policy of the business to depreciate motor vehicles by 20% per annum using the reducing-balance method.

Link

For more information on depreciation, see Chapter 4, page 63.

Calculate the depreciation charge on the motor vehicle for each of the years ended 31 December 2009, 2010 and 2011.

	Value of asset at beginning of year £	Depreciation calculation £	Depreciation charge £
2009	18,000	20% × £18,000	3,600
2010	14,400	20% × £14,400	2,880
2011	11,520	20% × £11,520	2,304

Table 7.1 *Calculating depreciation*

Activity

A business has a non-current asset that cost £100,000. If depreciation is provided annually at 20% using the reducing-balance method, calculate the depreciation charge in year 2.

How do the two methods of depreciation compare?

The straight-line method of depreciation:

■ is straightforward to calculate
■ results in an even depreciation charge each year.

The reducing-balance method of depreciation:

■ is more complex to calculate
■ results in a declining depreciation charge from one year to the next, which may reflect reality for certain assets
■ may result in a more even charge against profits each year for non-current assets if maintenance, repairs and servicing charges are considered alongside depreciation.

How to record depreciation in the ledger

Businesses keep separate records of the cost of each type of non-current asset and the accumulating depreciation on each type of non-current asset. So in the general ledger you are likely to find, for example, the following two accounts:

Machinery (at cost) Account

Provision for Depreciation of Machinery Account

At the end of each financial year the provision for depreciation account is updated with the annual depreciation charge. The double entry is as follows:

Dr Income Statement

Cr Provision for Depreciation Account

As a result the amount recorded in provision for depreciation account accumulates as the years go by, until the non-current asset is sold or scrapped.

Illustration

How to record depreciation in ledger accounts

Murray Traders purchased some machinery on 1 January 2009 for
£50,000. Machinery is depreciated by 20% per annum using the
straight-line method.

Record this information in the business's general ledger for the
years 2009, 2010 and 2011.

Step 1: Calculate the annual depreciation charge: 20% × cost
£50,000, i.e. £10,000

Step 2: Prepare two separate accounts for machinery in the general
ledger

Step 3: Record the purchase of machinery on 1 January 2009

Dr		Machinery at Cost Account					Cr
2009							
Jan	1	Bank	50,000				

Dr		Provision for Depreciation (Machinery) Account					Cr
2010				2009			
Dec	31	Balance c/d	20,000	Dec	31	Income statement	10,000
				2010			
				Dec	31	Income statement	10,000
			20,000	2011			20,000
2011				Jan	1	Balance b/d	20,000
Dec	31	Balance c/d	30,000	Dec	31	Income statement	10,000
			30,000				30,000
				2012			
				Jan	1	Balance b/d	30,000

Step 4: Record the first year's depreciation charge on 31 December 2009

Step 5: Record the depreciation charge for the year ended 31 December 2010 and balance the provision account

Step 6: Record the depreciation charge for the year ended 31 December 2011 and balance the provision account

Figure 7.10 *Recording depreciation in the ledger*

Activity

Does a provision for depreciation account have a debit or credit balance?

The sale of a non-current asset

How to record the sale of a non-current asset

When a non-current asset is sold, it will be necessary to:

- eliminate the original cost of the non-current assets from the ledger;
- eliminate the accumulated depreciation on that non-current asset;
- record the amount received for the non-current asset in the sale;
- assess whether a profit or loss was made on the sale of the asset.

The process involves the use of a 'non-current asset disposal account'. This
account will automatically show the profit or loss made on the sale as the
closing balance of the account. A profit will arise if the asset is sold for more
than its net book value; a loss will arise if the asset is sold for less than its
net book value. The profit or loss on disposal is transferred to the business's
income statement as a gain or a loss at the end of the financial period.

How to record the sale of a non-current asset

Murray Traders purchased some office equipment on 1 January 2009 for £12,000. The office equipment was depreciated by 25% per annum using the straight-line method on 31 December 2009 and 31 December 2010. The accounts recording this information are shown below.

On 17 May 2011 the office equipment was sold for £2,300 and a cheque received for this amount.

Record the disposal of the fixed asset in the business's ledger.

Step 1: Prepare an Office Equipment Disposal Account

Step 2: Transfer the cost of the office equipment to the disposal account

Step 3: Transfer the accumulated depreciation charge to the disposal account

Step 4: Record the receipt of the cheque in the disposal account

Step 5: Balance the disposal account. The balance will show automatically whether there is a loss or profit on the disposal that is transferred to the income statement.

Dr			Office Equipment at Cost				Cr
2009				2011			
Jan	1	Bank	12,000	May	17	Disposal	12,000

Dr			Provision For Depreciation (Office Equipment) Account				Cr
2010				2009			
Dec	31	Balance c/d	6,000	Dec	31	Income statement	3,000
				2010			
				Dec	31	Income statement	3,000
			6,000				6,000
2011				2011			
May	17	Disposal	6,000	Jan	1	Balance b/d	6,000

Dr			Office Equipment Disposal Account				Cr
2011				2011			
May	17	Disposal	12,000	May	17	Depreciation	6,000
					17	Bank	2,300
					17	Income statement (loss)	3,700
			12,000				12,000

Figure 7.11 *Recording the sale of a non-current asset*

Note: the loss will be recorded in the income statement as an extra cost for the year.

Learning outcomes

As a result of studying this topic, you should now be able to:
- define the key term depreciation
- explain why businesses depreciate their non-current assets
- calculate depreciation using both the straight-line and reducing-balance methods
- evaluate the two methods of calculating depreciation
- prepare a provision for depreciation account recording entries for depreciation over several years
- prepare a ledger account to record the disposal of a non-current asset

■ prepare financial statements that include depreciation of non-current
assets and the profit or loss on the disposal of a non-current asset

■ prepare statements of financial position (balance sheets) showing
information about non-current assets: cost, accumulated depreciation and
net book value

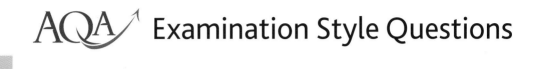 Examination Style Questions

1   The following information is available about a business's non-current assets.

Non-current (fixed) asset	Cost £	Depreciation Rate	Depreciation Method
Office equipment	18,500	20%	Straight line
Machinery	86,000	40%	Reducing balance

Calculate the depreciation charge on each non-current asset for Year 2.

2   On 1 January 2009 a business purchased a new delivery vehicle at a cost of £42,000. The business's
policy is to depreciate all vehicles by 30% per annum using the reducing balance method. The
business's financial year end is 31 December. Prepare the provision for depreciation of motor vehicles
account in the general ledger for each of the years 2009, 2010 and 2011. Balance the account at the
end of 2010 and 2011.

3   A business sold some fittings on 14 August 2011. The fittings had been purchased for £22,800 and had
a net book value of £8,300 at the date of disposal. A cheque for £4,200 was received for the fittings on
the date of sale. Prepare the fittings disposal account in the business's general ledger.

4   A business purchased some office equipment on 1 January 2009 for £14,000. The office equipment
has been depreciated by 40% per annum using the reducing balance method. The business's financial
year end is 31 December. The office equipment was sold on 28 September 2011 for £3,500 and
a cheque received for this amount on the date of sale. It is the business's policy to provide a full
year's depreciation in the year of sale. Prepare (i) the provision for depreciation of office equipment
account, and (ii) the office equipment disposal account in the business's general ledger.

5   Lucia Eve is the owner of Supatext Stationers. Her business's financial year ended on 31 December
2011 when the following trial balance was extracted from the business's books. The trading section of
the income statement had already been prepared.

	Dr £	Cr £
Bad debts	323	
Bank balance		871
Bank loan (repayable June 2012)		6,000
Bank loan interest	520	
Business rates	11,380	
Capital		333,000
Discounts	458	571
Drawings	38,500	
Electricity charges	6,310	
Equipment and furniture		
cost	24,000	
provision for depreciation 1 January 2011		9,600
Freehold premises		
cost	440,000	
provision for depreciation 1 January 2011		52,800
Gross profit		192,618
Inventory 31 December 2011	18,840	
Loss on the sale of furniture	790	
Motor vehicles		
cost	24,000	
provision for depreciation 1 January 2011		15,840
Provision for doubtful debts 1 January 2011		625
Rent received		8,280
Trade payables		14,336
Trade receivables	11,840	
Wages and salaries	57,580	
	634,541	634,541

Additional information at 31 December 2011

1 Electricity charges due but unpaid, £280

2 Business rates prepaid, £595

3 The tenant had paid three months' rent, £3,510 on 1 December 2011 covering the period 1 December 2011 to 29 February 2012

4 The provision for doubtful debts should be maintained at 5% of trade receivables (debtors)

5 Non-current assets should be depreciated as follows: freehold premises 2% per annum on cost; office equipment 20% per annum using the straight-line method; motor vehicles 40% per annum using the reducing balance method.

Prepare the income statement for the year ended 31 December 2011 and a statement of financial position (balance sheet) at that date.

4 Capital and revenue expenditure

Key terms

Capital expenditure: money spent on non-current assets that is intended to benefit future financial periods.

Revenue expenditure: money spent on running costs that benefits only the current financial period.

Understanding the terms revenue and capital expenditure

What is capital expenditure?

Put simply, **capital expenditure** is money spent on non-current assets.

A more sophisticated definition would mention that it is money spent that has a long-term benefit to a business.

Long term means more than one year.

Examples of capital expenditure:

The purchase of any non-current asset such as premises, machinery, equipment, vehicles, fixtures, fittings.

Money spent improving the non-current asset that adds value to the non-current asset, such as fitting storage racks to a delivery van, or decorating (as opposed to redecorating) a newly built extension to an office block.

Capital expenditure also includes money spent on acquiring non-current assets or making them available for use. Examples include: legal costs when purchasing premises, carriage costs when purchasing new office equipment, installation costs when installing a new machine. In each of these situations the argument is that the benefit from spending money on these costs is as long lasting as the non-current asset itself.

What is revenue expenditure?

Revenue expenditure refers to money spent on running costs. A more sophisticated definition would mention that it is money spent that has short-term benefit to a business, where short-term means less than one year. A feature of revenue expenditure is that it is recurring, i.e. has to be paid for again and again.

Examples of revenue expenditure:

Any expense such as wages, salaries, light and heat, rent, rates, insurance, etc.

Repairs, renewals, maintenance and servicing costs are also considered to be revenue expenditure. The argument is that these costs do not add any value to the non-current asset.

Applying the terms

Illustration

How to distinguish between revenue and capital expenditure

Murray Traders purchased a new delivery van. The following payments were made when the delivery van was purchased.

	£
Delivery van	17,400
Insurance of van	860
Adapting shelving to create more storage space	520
First tank of fuel	30
Road fund licence	160
Painting 'Murray Traders' and the business logo on sides of van	220

Table 7.2 *Delivery van payments*

Activity

Jim Murray has recently purchased some new equipment for Murray Traders. He has been told that the amount paid in wages to an employee who installed the new equipment should be added to the value of the equipment. Jim says he thought wages were an expense that was recorded in the income statement. Explain to Jim why, in this situation, wages should be added to the value of the equipment.

Calculate the total revenue expenditure and total capital expenditure.

Capital items are: delivery van; adapting shelving; painting name and logo.

Revenue items are: insurance; fuel, road fund licence

Capital: £17,400 + £520 + £220 = £18,140

Revenue: £860 + £30 + £160 = £1,050

Note: it follows from this calculation that the delivery van account should record £18,140 as the cost of the van and the annual depreciation charge should be based on this amount. The revenue expenditure of £1,050 should be charged to the income statement at the end of the financial period.

AQA Examiner's tip

The most common error with this topic is to mix up the definitions. To avoid this problem, find some way of linking capital expenditure with non-current assets, and revenue expenditure with running costs.

The importance of the distinction

Why does the distinction between capital and revenue expenditure matter?

Expenditure regarded as capital expenditure affects the figures shown for non-current assets on a statement of financial position (balance sheet).

Expenditure regarded as revenue expenditure affects the figures shown for expenses in a business's income statement.

If errors are made in classifying expenditure, it follows that non-current asset totals and profits figures will be inaccurate. If profit is inaccurate, the figure for capital on the statement of financial position (balance sheet) will also be inaccurate.

Non-current assets totals, profit and capital figures are all important for the managers or owners of businesses when analysing business performance. If the analysis is based on inaccurate information, it is likely that the managers or owners will draw incorrect conclusions and possibly make wrong decisions.

Learning outcomes

As a result of studying this topic, you should now be able to:

- explain the meaning of each of the terms capital and revenue expenditure and give examples of each

- apply your understanding of these terms to a variety of different situations

- calculate figures for total revenue and capital expenditure correctly selecting items from a list

- explain why the distinction between the two terms is important in preparing financial statements

- prepare financial statements that reflect the correct treatment of items of revenue and capital expenditure

AQA Examination Style Questions

1   (i) Contrast revenue and capital expenditure giving one example of each type of expenditure.
    (ii) Explain why it is important to distinguish accurately between these two types of expenditure.

2   In each of the following examples, state whether the amount spent is revenue expenditure or capital expenditure. Assume the business sells clothing.

	Expenditure	Type of expenditure: capital or revenue?
a	Upgrading of computer printer	
b	Printer cartridges	
c	Maintenance of computer equipment	
d	Redecoration of shop interior	
e	Additional sales counters	
f	Carriage paid on delivery of new sales counters	

3   On 1 January 2011 Sarah West purchased a new delivery van for use by her business. The van cost £18,400. In addition, Sarah has paid for additional shelving to be fitted in the van at a cost of £4,300. The business's name and an advertising slogan have also been painted on both sides of the van at a cost of £1,300. Sarah paid an annual insurance premium of £440 and road fund licence for 2011 of £200. The business's policy is to depreciate motor vehicles over a five-year period. Sarah expects the new delivery van to have a residual value of £2,500.

Use this information to calculate (i) the capital expenditure and (ii) the revenue expenditure for the year ended 31 December 2011.

8

Limited liability companies

Limited liability companies are a particularly important form of organisation because so many larger businesses in the UK are limited companies, and, as a result, a very significant amount of business activity in the British economy is conducted by this form of organisation. Many businesses that are familiar names to everyone are limited companies, including leading retailers such as Marks and Spencer plc and Littlewoods Ltd, food manufacturers such as Innocent Ltd, world-famous football clubs, such as Manchester United plc, and fast food chains, such as McDonald's UK, etc. In Chapter 5 you will already have learned about the advantages and disadvantages of forming a limited company. In this chapter you will learn about the more practical aspects of preparing the accounts of a limited company. You will find that many of the skills you have developed when preparing a sole trader's financial statements will be very useful as the basis of the work you are going to do on limited companies. For example, a limited company's income statement is very similar to that of a sole trader; the assets and liabilities that are to be found on a sole trader's statement of financial position (balance sheet) will also be found on the statement of financial position (balance sheet) of a limited company.

1   Financial statements

In this topic you will learn:

- many terms and features of limited companies

- how to prepare the financial statements of a limited company, including a statement of changes in equity that records dividends paid

- how to prepare the statement of financial position (balance sheet) of a limited company that takes account of current liabilities such as corporation tax, debenture interest due, non-current liabilities including debentures, and details of shares and reserves.

■ Understanding limited companies: the fundamentals

Here is a summary of the main points you need to know. Throughout, there are examples to support your understanding. Please note that, for convenience, 'limited liability companies' are often referred to as 'limited companies'.

Who owns a limited company?

Limited liability companies are owned by **shareholders,** each of whom has an investment (shareholding) in the company. Shareholders are sometimes referred to as members of the company. Shareholders do not take part in the day-to-day running of a company unless they also happen to be **directors** of the company. Shareholders' involvement with the running of a company is normally limited to attending an **annual general meeting**. Since shares usually have voting rights, shareholders can vote for the election of individual directors at the annual general meeting (AGM).

Why 'limited liability'?

Limited liability in the title of a company means the company has limited liability for the debts of the business. Shareholders can lose their investment if the company fails but no more than that. Unlike a sole trader (or partner in a partnership) the private possessions of a shareholder cannot be used to settle the outstanding debts of a failing company. Strictly speaking shareholders have responsibility for the debts of the company to the extent they have invested, or agreed to invest, in the company.

Types of limited company

Limited companies are primarily of two types: private and public companies.

Private companies have the abbreviation 'Ltd' in their title. Those entitled to become shareholders in private companies are restricted to the individuals who established the company, their families and friends, and employees of the company. In other words, general members of the public cannot be shareholders and it is not possible to buy shares in a private limited company on a stock exchange. There must be at least one shareholder in a private limited company.

Illustration

Zextra Ltd: an example of a private limited company

Zextra Ltd is a private limited company. The founders of the company, David and Sandra Ratcliffe, are the major shareholders having invested a considerable amount of money. However, some relations and friends have also invested in shares. All these shareholders are aware that they could lose the amount they have invested if the company is unsuccessful, but appreciate that this is the maximum they can lose.

Public companies have the abbreviation 'plc' in their title. As the title suggests, members of the public may invest in these companies. Shareholders often come from a wide range of investors including private individuals and 'institutional investors'. Institutional investors include other companies (for example, banks and insurance companies); some of the pension funds built up by other institutions may be invested in public limited companies. Public companies must have at least two shareholders and there is no limit on the maximum number of shareholders. Public companies tend to be very large scale organisations and they must have a share capital of at least £50,000 (there is no such requirement for a private limited company).

Shares and dividends

There are two (main) types of share: ordinary and preference. All shares are of a particular denomination. The usual face value (**par** or **nominal value**) of a share is £1, but some shares have a face value of 50p, £5, etc.

Ordinary shares (called **equity shares**) are the most common type of share. The owners of ordinary shares receive a dividend that varies depending on the amount of the company's profits. These are the owners who are the risk takers. Usually each ordinary share carries one vote. Ordinary shareholders, because they have votes, are able to control a limited company.

Preference shareholders receive a fixed dividend. The term '**preference shares**' is used for these shares because they rank before ordinary shareholders for the payment of dividends, i.e. are paid before ordinary shareholders. Because preference shareholders receive a fixed dividend, they are seen as taking less risk than ordinary shareholders who may do well or badly depending on how successful the company is. Normally preference shareholders do not have voting rights.

Link

For more information on limited companies, see Chapter 5, page 81.

Case study

Zextra Ltd

Zextra Ltd commenced trading on 1 January 2009. It has two directors, David Ratcliffe and his wife Sandra, who were responsible for establishing the company. The company specialises in providing high-quality organic soups made from the finest ingredients.

Key terms

Shareholders: the owners of a limited liability company.

Directors: are the senior managers of a limited company; they are appointed by shareholders at the AGM.

Annual general meeting: often called the AGM, is the yearly company meeting that can be attended by shareholders.

Private company: one in which only the founders of the company, their family, friends and employees can invest in shares.

Public company: one in which any member of the public can invest as shares are floated on the open market.

Ordinary shares: shares that carry voting rights and have a variable dividend that is dependent on the amount of profits.

Par value; nominal value: the face value of a share.

Equity shares: are ordinary shares.

Preference shares: shares that have a fixed rate of dividend and normally have no voting rights.

In the event of a company failing (going into 'liquidation'), preference shareholders have a prior claim over ordinary shareholders in regard to the repayment of capital.

Shareholders received dividends when there are profits available for distribution. A company that has no profits or revenue reserves (see below) cannot pay any dividends.

Authorised and issued capital

Limited companies have an 'authorised' and 'issued' capital. **Authorised capital** is the maximum value of shares that the company can issue. Those who form the company decide this figure right at the outset, but they can increase the authorised capital at a later date if they so wish. The **issued capital** is the value of the shares that have already been issued; it will be equal to, or less than, the authorised capital.

Illustration

Using the basic terms associated with limited companies

Zextra Ltd has an authorised capital made up of 100,000 6% preference shares of £1 each and 900,000 ordinary shares of 50p each. The issued capital is made up of all the preference shares and 600,000 ordinary shares.

What this means is as follows:

The face value of the Zextra Ltd's shares is: £1 (preference shares); 50p (ordinary shares)

The total potential (authorised) capital of the company is £550,000 (Preference shares £100,000 + Ordinary shares £450,000).

The total issued capital is £400,000 (Preference Shares £100,000 + £300,000 Ordinary shares).

The preference shareholders are entitled to receive a fixed dividend of 6%. This would amount to £6,000 per annum (i.e. 6% × the issued preference share capital of £100,000).

The ordinary shareholders will receive a dividend based on the issued ordinary share capital of £300,000. The amount of the dividend will depend on the profits made by the company and the directors' decisions about how best to use the profits.

Activity

Stephen and Carole were the founder members of the private limited company called Beltramina Ltd. They planned that the company should have a maximum shareholding of 1m ordinary shares of £1 each and 200,000 7% preference shares of £1 each. Initially, shareholders were able to purchase 400,000 ordinary shares and 150,000 preference shares. State the following:

- the face value of the shares
- the amount of the company's authorised capital
- the amount of the company's issued capital
- the dividend that preference shares will hope to receive each year.

What happens to a company's profits?

A company's profits are subject to tax. Companies pay **corporation tax** to HM Revenue and Customs. (Note: sole traders and partnerships pay income tax to HM Revenue and Customs.) Corporation tax is deducted from the annual profit and becomes a current liability payable nine months after the end of the company's financial year.

Profits after tax belong to the company's shareholders. However, it is the directors who decide how the profits should be distributed. They can choose between distributing profits as dividends and retained profits within the company. Retained profits are usually referred to as **retained earnings** and form what are called the **revenue reserves** of the company.

When directors decide to retain profits this benefits the company because it means that cash that would have been paid out as dividends can now be spent on other things. In fact the cash will probably already have been spent.

Illustration

The directors of Zextra Ltd make decisions about the company's first year profits

Zextra Ltd made a profit of £160,000 during its first year of trading, i.e. for the year ending 31 December 2009. The company's accountant has told the two directors, David and Sandra Ratcliffe, that making a profit does not mean that there is this amount of money stored away in the company's bank account. The accountant has gone on to explain that much of the extra wealth that has been created as a result of making a profit is now tied up in inventories, receivables, additional non-current assets and so on. During the year, the directors have already paid the preference share dividend of £6,000 and, aware that the company was performing reasonably well, have also paid a dividend of 10p per share on the ordinary shares. The ordinary share dividend amounted to £60,000 (ie 10p × 600,000 ordinary shares). The directors are aware that part of the profits will be subject to corporation tax, which they must pay by 30 September 2010.

Preparing a company's financial statements

Illustration

Prepare Zextra Ltd's financial statements

The following summarised details have been extracted from the books of Zextra Ltd at the end of its second year of trading, 31 December 2010.

	£
Auditors' fees	5,200
Depreciation of non-current assets	35,000
Dividends paid	
Ordinary shares	45,000
Preference shares	6,000
Directors' fees	63,300
Gross profit	296,400
Interest charges	7,500

Key terms

Retained earnings: undistributed profits arising from the normal course of business.

Revenue reserves: profits that arise from everyday trading activities and can be distributed as dividends.

Corporation tax: tax on a company's profits.

AQA Examiner's tip

It is a common mistake to find candidates writing about 'spending profits'. In this context, it is only money that can be spent. It is preferable to use an expression such as 'profits were used to finance the payment of dividends'.

Issued capital

600,000 ordinary shares of 50p each	300,000
100,000 6% preference shares of £1 each	100,000
Operating expenses	72,800
Retained earnings at 1 January 2010	54,000

Prepare the company's end of year financial statements: income statement for the year ended 31 December 2010 and statement of changes in equity for the year ended 31 December 2010. Provision should be made for corporation tax of £34,500.

Explanatory notes

Auditors' fees: all but the smallest limited companies are required to have their accounts audited. The auditors check that the accounts present a true and fair view of the company's affairs. Auditors are appointed by, and report to, the shareholders of a company. Auditors' fees (sometimes called auditors' remuneration) should be treated as an expense.

Directors' fees: these are amounts paid to directors for the work they do in running the company (sometimes called directors' remuneration or directors' emoluments). Directors' fees should also be treated as an expense.

Retained earnings at 1 January 2010: companies do not usually distribute all their profits, so a balance remains of undistributed profits. This balance is carried forward from one year to the next. It can be distributed as dividends at any time the directors feel this would be wise. Normally, in successful companies retained earnings steadily accumulate over the years. Retained earnings are shown on the company's statement of financial position (balance sheet) (see below).

Here, first of all, is the profit and loss section of Zextra Ltd's income statement for the year under review.

ZEXTRA LTD		
Income Statement for the year ended 31 December 2010		
	£	£
Gross profit		296,400
Less: auditors' fees	5,200	
depreciation of non-current assets	35,000	
directors' fees	63,300	
operating expenses	72,800	
		176,300
Operating profit		120,100
Less: finance charges*		13,500
Profit before taxation		106,600
Less: corporation tax		34,500
Profit after taxation		72,100

*Note: finance charges includes interest on loans (£7,500) and also preference share dividends paid (6,000).

Additional explanatory notes

Operating profit: it is useful to show a clearly labelled subtotal for profit before deducting any financial charges such as interest and preference share dividends paid. Operating profit is used in some important ratio calculations used to assess the performance of a company (see Chapter 9).

Profit before/after taxation: profit before taxation is the operating profit less **finance charges**; profit after taxation is the company's profit less provision for corporation tax.

Companies are required to prepare a **Statement of Changes in Equity** which shows changes in a company's retained earnings, shares and any reserves during a year. Part of this statement replaces the profit and loss appropriation account which used to be prepared by limited companies and to which you may find reference in some textbooks and past examination papers.

Here is an extract from the company's Statement of Changes in Equity for the year under review dealing with retained earnings and dividends paid.

ZEXTRA LTD	
Statement of Changes in Equity (Extract) for the year ended 31 December 2010	
	£
Retained earnings at 1 January 2010	54,000
Profit for the year after taxation	72,100
	126,100
Share dividend paid	(45,000)
Retained earnings at 31 December 2010	81,100

The extract shows how retained earnings have changed during the year. The entries are always in the sequence:

1st	Retained earnings at beginning of year
2nd	Add profit (or deduct loss) after taxation
3rd	Deduct ordinary share dividends paid
4th	Retained earnings at end of year

There is more about Statement of Changes in Equity on page 122.

Preparing a company's statement of financial position (balance sheet)

Illustration

Zextra's statement of financial position (balance sheet) at 31 December 2011

On 31 December 2011 the following balances remained in the books of Zextra Ltd after the preparation of the income statement and statement of changes in equity for the year ended on that date.

Key terms

Operating profit: profit before deducting any financial charges such as interest.

Finance charges: include interest on loans and preferences share dividends paid.

Profit before taxation: operating profit less interest charges

Profit after taxation: profit less provision for corporation tax.

Statement of Changes in Equity: forms part of the end of year financial statements of a limited company and details changes that have taken place during the financial year in the company's issued share capital and reserves.

Background knowledge

Companies no longer have to record 'proposed dividends' in their end of year financial statements. Proposed dividends are the directors' suggestions to shareholders about dividends which are to be paid at some future date. Only dividends actually paid are shown in the accounts (as in the illustration above). You may find reference to proposed dividends in some past examination papers and textbooks.

	Dr	Cr
	£	£
Accruals		2,000
Cash and cash equivalents	9,000	
Corporation tax due		44,000
Inventory	42,000	
Issued shares		
ordinary shares of 50p each		300,000
6% preference shares of £1 each		100,000
Non-current assets		
cost	590,000	
provision for depreciation		125,000
Prepayments	1,000	
Retained earnings		60,000
Trade payables		28,000
Trade receivables	17,000	
	659,000	659,000

Here is the company's statement of financial position (balance sheet) based on this trial balance.

Zextra Ltd			
Statement of financial position (Balance Sheet) at 31 December 2011			
	£	£	£
NON-CURRENT ASSETS	Cost	Total Depreciation	Net
	590,000	125,000	465,000
CURRENT ASSETS			
Inventory	42,000		
Trade receivables	17,000		
Prepayments	1,000		
Cash and cash equivalents	9,000		
		69,000	
Less CURRENT LIABILITIES			
Trade payables	28,000		
Corporation tax due	44,000		
Accruals	2,000		
		74,000	
NET CURRENT LIABILITIES			(5,000)
			460,000
EQUITY			
Authorised share capital			
900,000 ordinary shares of 50p each			450,000
100,000 6% preference shares of £1 each			100,000

Issued share capital			
600,000 ordinary shares of 50p each			300,000
100,000 6% preference shares of £1 each			100,000
Retained earnings			60,000
			460,000

Explanatory notes

Cash and cash equivalents: on company statements of financial position (balance sheets) this item represents cash and bank balances. The item may appear as a current liability if the bank balance is overdrawn and the overdraft exceeds any cash in hand.

Corporation tax due: corporation tax is payable within nine months of the end of a company's financial year and so is recorded as a current liability.

Net current liabilities: is the label used when the subtotal for current liabilities exceeds the subtotal for current assets. Alternatively, if the net figure is positive the subtotal should be labelled net current assets.

Equity: is the overall heading for the second part of the statement of financial position (balance sheet). Equity includes shares and reserves. If known, the authorised capital can be noted on the statement of financial position (balance sheet). You will see that ordinary shares should precede preference shares and shares precede any reserves (here, just the retained earnings figure).

Understanding limited companies: additional matters

Here are some additional points that will help you develop an understanding of limited liability companies.

Debentures

Debentures are loans, and as such are part of the non-current liabilities of a company. It is important to avoid confusing debentures (liabilities) and ordinary and preference shares (capital). A debenture is technically the name of the document recording details of the loan.

Debentures carry a fixed rate of interest that is usually paid in two six-monthly instalments. Debenture interest is an ordinary expense of a company and so it is charged to the income statement.

Debenture holders are repaid ahead of shareholders in the event of a company failure. It is possible that the loan will be secured on a non-current asset (example: freehold property). In this case the proceeds of the sale of the non-current asset are used to repay the loan should the company go into liquidation, or to pay debenture interest if this has not been paid.

Debentures are usually repayable at some future date specified in the title: for example 8% Debentures 2022, means that the loan carries interest of 8% per annum and is repayable in the year 2022. Debentures should be recorded under the heading non-current liabilities on the company's statement of financial position (balance sheet).

> **Key terms**
>
> **Cash and cash equivalents:** a company's cash and bank balances.
>
> **Net current liabilities:** the difference between current liabilities and current assets where current liabilities exceed current assets.
>
> **Equity:** a company's capital made up of shares and reserves.
>
> **Debentures:** loans to a limited company on which a fixed rate of interest is paid. The interest is shown as an expense in the income statement.

Shareholders' funds

'**Shareholders' funds**' is a term often used to describe the total of issued capital and reserves.

Activity

Metrix plc is partly financed by 7% debentures (repayable 2020) totalling £850,000 that were issued in 2010. During the year ended 31 December 2011 the debenture holders have been paid £29,750 in debenture interest.

a How much debenture interest should be recorded in the company's income statement for the year ended 31 December 2011.

b How much debenture interest should be shown in the company's statement of financial position (balance sheet) at 31 December 2011.

Share premium

Once a company is established the transfer or market value of its ordinary shares will vary. For example if the original par (face or nominal) value of a share was £1 its value will increase as the company builds up retained earnings. If the company makes a fresh issue of shares, the law permits it to offer these shares at a price in excess of the par value. The extra amount is called the **share premium**.

The share premium is a reserve. On a company statement of financial position (balance sheet) it should be placed after the share capital but before the retained earnings. The share premium is regarded as a **capital reserve**. This technical term is used to describe any gain made by a company which did not arise from normal trading activities. The Companies Acts forbid capital reserves to be used to finance cash dividends to shareholders.

Details of a share issue at a premium should be shown in the statement of changes in equity for the year in which the issue occurred.

Interim dividends

Companies can pay dividends just once a year or half-yearly. Half-yearly dividends are known as **interim dividends**. In the case of the preference shareholders, they may receive their fixed dividend in one payment, or divided into two equal payments received at six monthly intervals. In the case of ordinary shareholders, they may receive an interim dividend and an additional final dividend in one year. Only dividends actually paid are recorded in the company's accounts.

Key terms

Shareholders' funds: the total of issued capital and reserves.

Share premium: the amount paid for a share above its face value

Capital reserve: profits that have arisen from non-trading activities which may not be used to finance the payment of cash dividends.

Interim dividend: a dividend paid half way through a financial year.

Illustration

Zextra Ltd issues debentures and shares at a premium

The directors of Zextra Ltd decided that it was a good time for the company to expand. It was agreed that the 300,000 remaining ordinary shares should be issued. The face value of the shares was, of course, 50p. However, the directors decided that in view of the company's success they should be issued at 75p each. In addition, it was agreed that the company should borrow £50,000 by issuing 7% debentures redeemable in 2020. These transactions took place on 1 January 2012.

The results of these decisions were as follows:

Shares: the issued share capital of company increased by 300,000 × 50p ordinary shares (i.e. £150,000).

Share premium: each share issued raised an additional 25p because they were issued at 75p each. The total amount of the share premium was 300,000 × 25p, ie £75,000.

The total cash raised by the share issue was £225,000.

Debentures: the debenture issue raised £50,000. The debentures are shown as a non-current liability on the company's statement of financial position (balance sheet).

Debenture interest: each year the company must pay debenture holders interest of £3,500 (i.e. 7% × £50,000). The interest is charged to the income statement.

Activity

The directors of Causerton Ltd have decided to issue 120,000 ordinary shares with a face value of £1 each at a price of £2.10 per share.

a Calculate the amount of the share premium.

b Calculate the total cash to be raised by the share issue.

Preparing a company's end of year financial statements

Illustration

Preparing Zextra Ltd's end of year financial statements

Zextra Ltd's income statement for the year ended 31 December 2012 had already been prepared. The following balances remained in the company's books.

	Dr	Cr
	£	£
Accruals		3,000
Cash and cash equivalents	25,000	
Corporation tax due		73,000
7% Debentures (2020)		50,000
Dividends paid (interim)		
ordinary shares	30,000	
Dividends paid (final)		
ordinary shares	60,000	
Inventory	37,000	
Issued shares		
ordinary shares		450,000
preference shares		100,000
Non-current assets		
cost	1,000,000	
provision for depreciation		240,000
Prepayments	6,000	
Profit for year after tax		90,000
Retained earnings at 1 January 2012		60,000
Share premium		75,000
Trade payables		36,000
Trade receivables	19,000	
	1,183,000	1,183,000

Note: the trial balance does not include any reference to preference share dividends, because they would already have been deducted from the income statement.

Here is the company's statement of changes in equity for the year.

Zextra Ltd					
Statement of Changes in Equity for the year ended 31 December 2012					
	Ordinary Shares	Preference Shares	Share Premium	Retained Earnings	Total
	£	£	£	£	£
At 1 January 2012	300,000	100,000		60,000	460,000
Share issue	150,000		75,000		225,000
Profit for year				90,000	90,000
Dividends paid					
interim				(30,000)	(30,000)
final				(60,000)	(60,000)
At 31 December 2012	450,000	100,000	75,000	60,000	685,000

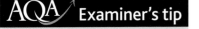

AQA Examiner's tip

If you are asked to present a full statement of changes in equity, don't forget to include a total column.

Explanatory note

This is a full version of a statement of changes in equity. It shows changes not just in retained earnings, but in each type of share and in each reserve. Note that the correct layout includes a total column.

And here is the company's statement of financial position (balance sheet).

Zextra Ltd			
Statement of financial position (Balance Sheet) at 31 December 2012			
	£	£	£
NON-CURRENT ASSETS	Cost	Total Depreciation	Net
	1,000,000	240,000	760,000
CURRENT ASSETS			
Inventory	37,000		
Trade receivables	19,000		
Prepayments	6,000		
Cash and cash equivalents	25,000		
		87,000	
less CURRENT LIABILITIES			
Trade payables	36,000		
Corporation tax due	73,000		
Accruals	3,000		
		112,000	
NET CURRENT LIABILITIES			(25,000)
			735,000

NON-CURRENT LIABILITIES			
7% Debentures (2020)			50,000
			685,000
EQUITY			
Authorised and issued shares			
900,000 ordinary shares of 50p each			450,000
100,000 6% preference shares of £1 each			100,000
Share premium			75,000
Retained earnings			60,000
			685,000

Learning outcomes

As a result of studying this topic, you should now be able to:

- define a wide range of terms associated with limited companies

- prepare the income statement of a limited company including entries for debenture interest, auditors' remuneration and directors fees

- prepare an income statement identifying the subtotal for operating profit, profit before taxation, profit after taxation

- prepare a statement of changes in equity showing how shares and reserves have changed during a financial period

- prepare the statement of financial position (balance sheet) of a limited company to include additional liabilities such as corporation tax due and debenture interest due, non-current liabilities such as debentures, and an equity section showing shares and reserves including share premium and retained earnings

AQA↗ Examination Style Questions

1   The following information has been taken from the books of KDK Ltd at the end of its financial year, 31 October 2011.

	£
Auditors' remuneration	11,200
Depreciation of non-current assets	48,900
Directors' fees	84,700
Dividends paid	110,000
Gross profit	295,000
Interest charges	14,300
Operating expenses	29,600
Retained earnings at 1 November 2010	76,100

Additional information

Provision should be made for corporation tax of £53,500.

Prepare the company's income statement and an extract from the statement of changes in equity showing retained earnings for the year ended 31 October 2011.

2   The following balances remained in the books of Barbary Ltd before the preparation of the company's income statement and statement of changes in equity at 31 December 2011.

	Dr £	Cr £
Accruals		5,000
Cash and cash equivalents	11,000	
Corporation tax due		38,600
Inventory	19,200	
Issued capital		
ordinary shares of £1 each		500,000
8% preference shares of £1 each		60,000
Non-current assets		
cost	845,000	
provision for depreciation		118,600
Prepayments	2,000	
Provision for doubtful debts		700
Retained earnings		151,800
Trade payables		19,900
Trade receivables	17,400	
	894,600	894,600

Additional information

The company's authorised capital consists of 1,000,000 ordinary shares of £1 each and 200,000 8% preference shares of £1 each.

Prepare the company's statement of financial position (balance sheet) at 31 December 2011.

3   On 1 January 2011, the following balances appeared in the books of Ackley Products Ltd.

	£
Issued capital: 800,000 ordinary shares of 50p each	400,000
Retained earnings	178,400
Share premium	80,000

On 1 January 2011 the company issued a further 500,000 ordinary shares of 50p each. These shares were issued at 80p each, and all the shares were taken up.

During the year ended 31 December 2011 the directors paid a dividend of 5p per share on all the ordinary shares.

The company made a profit after tax of £148,000 during the year ended 31 December 2011.

Prepare the company's statement of changes in equity for the year ended 31 December 2011.

4   Caverton Ltd has an authorised capital of 900,000 50p ordinary shares and 160,000 7% preference shares of £1 each. All the preference shares and 500,000 of the ordinary shares had been issued some years ago. On 31 December 2010 the balance of the company's share premium account was £60,000.

On 1 January 2011 the directors put into effect plans to expand the company by issuing the remaining ordinary shares at a premium of 30p per share. On the same day an issue of 8% debentures was made to raise £200,000.

On 31 December 2011 the following information was available.

	£
Administration expenses	23,200
Auditors' remuneration	8,000
Corporation tax provision for the year ended 31 December 2011	49,500
Debenture interest paid	8,000
Depreciation of non-current assets	68,100
Directors' fees	56,200
Dividends paid	See note below
Gross profit	310,800
Retained earnings at 1 January 2011	109,600
Selling and distribution expenses	18,400

Additional information

- Administration expenses of £3,800 were prepaid at 31 December 2011.
- Debenture interest is paid half-yearly on 15 June and 15 January.
- A full year's dividend was paid on the preference shares and a dividend of 5p per share was paid to ordinary shareholders, during the year ended 31 December 2011.

Prepare the company's income statement and statement of changes in equity for the year ended 31 December 2011.

5   The following balances were extracted from the books of YPX Ltd on 30 September 2011 after the business's operating profit for the year had been calculated.

	Dr £	Cr £
Cash and cash equivalents		8,460
Debenture interest due	14,400	
8% Debentures (2025)		360,000
Dividends paid	180,000	
Inventory	23,280	
Issued shares: 1,200,000 ordinary shares of £1 each		1,200,000
Non-current assets		
cost	2,300,000	
provision for depreciation		175,000
Operating profit		274,360
Retained earnings at 1 October 2010		185,940
Share premium		320,000
Trade payables		32,910
Trade receivables	38,990	
	2,556,670	2,556,670

Additional information

- Debenture interest for the second half year was due but unpaid.
- Provision should be made for corporation tax of £63,770.
- During the year the directors had made an issue of 400,000 ordinary shares of £1 each. The shares had been issued at £1.50 per share. The figures shown in the trial balance above take account of this information.

Complete the company's income statement and prepare the statement of changes in equity for the year ended 30 September 2011. Prepare the company's statement of financial position (balance sheet) at 30 September 2011.

2 Some more advanced matters

In this topic you will learn:

- about the revaluation of non-current assets

- how to record rights issues of shares

- how to record bonus issues of shares

- prepare statements of changes in equity and statements of financial position (balance sheets) to record revaluations, rights and/or bonus issues

Activity

The directors of a limited company have decided to revalue freehold property at £2.9m. The freehold property is currently valued at a net book value of £2.1m. Identify the effects of this revaluation on the company's statement of financial position (balance sheet).

Case Study

Harriton Ltd

Harriton Ltd is a well-established company with an authorised capital of 8m ordinary shares of £1 each. On 1 January 2008 the company's issued capital consisted of 3m ordinary shares. Harriton Ltd produces air conditioning units for use in commercial and industrial properties.

■ The revaluation of non-current assets

How does a revaluation of non-current assets affect a company's statement of financial position (balance sheet)?

The directors of a company can revalue a non-current asset upwards if they feel that its statement of financial position (balance sheet) value is significantly different from its market value. Upward valuations are most often applied to freehold land and buildings.

When a revaluation takes place the effect on the statement of financial position (balance sheet) is as follows:

Non-current assets: increase by the amount of the revaluation.

Revaluation reserve: appears on the list of reserves (after share premium and before retained earnings) by the amount of the (upwards) revaluation.

The double-entry for a revaluation is: Debit Non-current asset; Credit Revaluation reserve.

The increase in the value of a non-current asset is, of course, a gain for the company. However, this gain must not be shown in the company's income statement and it must not be used to finance any cash dividends. These legal restrictions arise because there is no cash to support to the increase in value. In other words, the revaluation reserve is, like the share premium, a capital reserve.

■ Rights issues

What is a rights issue of shares?

This is an issue of shares by a company designed to raise cash, but it has some special features to get round some of the problems that can arise from making a share issue to the general public. These potential problems are as follows:

- there can be no guarantee that the share issue will prove attractive to potential investors

- share issues are expensive because they can involve the use of specialist financial institutions to manage the issue

The directors of a company can try to get round these potential problems by offering the shares to existing shareholders. Shareholders are offered additional shares in proportion to their existing shareholding. For example, a rights issue might be described as a 'one for three' issue, meaning that a shareholder is offered one additional share for every three shares currently held. These shareholders have the right to take up the offer or to sell the shares to a third party – hence the term 'rights' issue. Offering shares to existing shareholders is less expensive than issuing shares to the general public. Furthermore, rights issues can be more successful than a general issue. This is because the directors are likely to offer the shares at a favourable price, below the price that otherwise would have to be paid to acquire shares in the company.

There is a possible additional benefit: because new shares are offered to existing shareholders, the control of the company is likely to remain with the same individuals as before. (This may not be quite the case, of course, if existing shareholders sell their rights to third parties.)

How does a rights issue affect the end of year financial statements?

A rights issue will be detailed in the statement of changes in equity and affect the company's statement of financial position (balance sheet) in the same way as any issue of shares. The items affected will be:

Cash and cash equivalents: will increase by the total cash raised by the issue

Issued shares: will increase by the face value of shares

Share premium: will increase will the additional amount raised by the share issue above the face value of the shares

Illustration

Revaluations and rights issues

The directors of Harriton Ltd made the following decisions to take effect on 31 December 2009.

- To revalue freehold property by £900,000 to £3,400,000.
- To make a right issue of ordinary shares: ordinary shareholders were offered 3 shares for every 5 shares currently held. There shares were offered at a price of £1.80 each. The rights issue was fully subscribed.

Immediately before these decisions came into effect the company's trial balance was as follows:

	Dr	Cr
	£000	£000
Cash and cash equivalents	45	
Current assets (except cash)	127	
Current liabilities		88
Freehold property	2,500	
Issued shares		
3m ordinary shares of £1 each		3,000
Other non-current assets	1,264	
Retained earnings		248
Share premium		600
	3,936	3,936

Here is an extract from the company's statement of changes in equity showing the rights issue and the company's statement of changes in equity (balance sheet) showing the effect of the revaluation and the rights issue.

Statement of Changes in Equity (Extract) for the year ended 31 December 2009		
	Ordinary Shares	Share Premium
	£000	£000
Before rights issue	3,000	600
Rights issue	1,800	1,440
After rights issue	4,800	2,040

Workings (rights issue) (figures in £000s)

Issued shares: 3 for 5 shares offered: i.e. $\frac{3}{5} \times 3,000$ shares = 1,800 shares of £1 each

Share premium: $1,800 \times 80p$ premium = £1,440

Cash received: $1,800 \times £1.80 = £3,240$

HARRITON LTD (Summarised) Statement of financial position (Balance Sheet) at 31 December 2009			
	£000	£000	£000
NON-CURRENT ASSETS			
Freehold property at valuation		3,400	
Other non-current assets		1,264	
			4,664
NON-CURRENT ASSETS	127		
Cash and cash equivalents	3,285		
		3,412	
Less CURRENT LIABILITIES		88	
Net current assets			3,324
			7,988
EQUITY			
Ordinary shares (4.8m)			4,800
Share premium			2,040
Revaluation reserve			900
Retained earnings			248
			7,988

Explanatory notes (figures in £000s)

1 Items shown in bold have changed their value since the trial balance
2 Revaluation:
   ▪ Add £900,000 to the value of freehold property so that it now appears at £3,400. The asset is clearly labelled 'at valuation'.

- Include a revaluation reserve of £900,000 immediately following the share premium. Capital reserves always precede revenue reserves.

3 Rights issue:

- Increase cash and cash equivalents by the amount received (£45 + £3,240)
- Increase ordinary shares by the face value of the shares issued (£3,000 + £1,800)
- Increase the share premium by the rights issue premium (£600 + £1,440)

Key terms

Rights issues: an issue of shares for cash where the existing shareholders are offered the right to buy the shares, usually at a favourable price.

Bonus issues

What is a bonus issue?

A **bonus issue** occurs when the directors of a company decide to change the structure of the company's statement of financial position (balance sheet), increasing share capital at the same time as reducing reserves. Unlike a rights issue, there is no cash involved in a bonus issue. It is a technical alteration to the components making up the equity section of the statement of financial position (balance sheet). Bonus issues, sometimes called scrip issues, often occur when the issued capital and reserves elements become unbalanced. In these situations issued shares are rather small in value, compared to the reserves which have built up over the years, and tend to be out of step with the company's permanent assets. Shareholders receive additional shares, but do not make any payment for them. A 'two for three' bonus issue, for example, would mean that a shareholder would receive two additional shares for every three shares currently held.

At first sight it sounds as if a bonus issue will be a considerable advantage to shareholders because they will own additional shares. However, the market price of shares will adjust in proportion to the change in issued shares.

Activity

A company has an issued capital consisting of 1.5m ordinary shares of £1 each. The directors are now proposing to make a rights issue and will offer existing shareholders 5 shares for every 3 currently held. The shares will be offered at a favourable price of £2.10 per share. Assuming the rights issue is successful, calculate

a the cash received from the rights issue

b the increase in the share premium arising from the rights issue.

Key terms

Bonus issue: the issue of additional shares to shareholders in proportion to their existing shareholding. No cash is paid for the additional shares. The issue is financed from the company's reserves, resulting in a restructuring of the equity section of the statement of financial position (balance sheet).

Illustration

Adjusting the market price of a share when a bonus issue takes place

Rachel owned 1,000 shares in a company. On 1 August 2011 the market price of the shares was £8 each.

So on 1 August 2011, Rachel's shareholding was worth £8,000.

On 2 August 2011 the company made a bonus issue of one share for every 4 shares currently held. So, Rachel looked forward to receiving an additional 250 shares (i.e. $\frac{1}{4} \times 1000$ shares), but she noticed that the market price of fell to £6.40 per share.

So on 2 August 2011, Rachel held 1,250 shares with a market price of £6.40, i.e. £8,000.

In this illustration the increase in shareholding was counterbalanced by the decrease in the market price of the shares.

If the share price does not quite fall in proportion to the bonus issue, however, there will be a financial advantage to the shareholder, and this quite often happens. Shareholders may also gain for the following reasons.

■ The shares become more marketable after a bonus issue, because the reduced market price makes the shares seem more attractive to potential investors.

■ If the directors of the company maintain the usual rate of dividend, then shareholders will gain because they will receive more in the way of dividends: they will receive dividends on their original shareholding plus dividends on the bonus shares.

How does a bonus issue affect the end of year financial statements?

A bonus issue will need to be recorded in the statement of changes in equity and it will also affect the equity section of the statement of financial position (balance sheet) as follows:

Issued shares: increase by the value of the bonus issue

Reserves: reduce by the value of the bonus issue

Any reserve can be used to finance a bonus issue. Often the opportunity is taken to use capital reserves, such as the share premium and/or revaluation reserve. If capital reserves are used rather than revenue reserves, the directors can be said to be 'maximising flexibility in regard to the payment of cash dividends', since only revenue reserves can be used to finance cash dividends.

Illustration

The effect of a bonus issue on end of year financial statements

On 31 December 2011 the following trial balance was extracted from the books of Harriton Ltd.

	Dr	Cr
	£000	£000
Cash and cash equivalents	82	
Current assets (except cash)	331	
Current liabilities		109
Freehold property at valuation	3,400	
Issued shares		
4.8m ordinary shares of £1 each		4,800
Other non-current assets	8,256	
Retained earnings		4,220
Revaluation reserve		900
Share premium		2,040
	12,069	12,069

The directors decided to make a bonus issue of 2 shares for every 3 shares currently held. The directors also decided to maintain maximum flexibility in regard to the financing of cash dividends.

Here is an extract from the company's statement of changes in equity recording the bonus issue.

	Ordinary Shares	Share Premium	Revaluation Reserve	Retained Earnings	Total
Statement of Changes in Equity (Extract) for the year ended 31 December 2011					
	£000	£000	£000	£000	£000
Before bonus issue	4,800	2,040	900	4,220	11,960
Bonus issue	3,200	(2,040)	(900)	(260)	0
After bonus issue	8,000	0	0	3,960	11,960

Workings (figures are in £000s)

Share issue: 2 for every 3 currently held $= \frac{2}{3} \times 4,800 = 3,200$ shares of £1 each

Financing of bonus issue: capital reserves to be used first (share premium £2,040 and revaluation reserve £900, total £2,940) leaving £260 to be found from revenue reserves (ie retained earnings).

HARRITON LTD			
(Summarised) Statement of financial position (Balance Sheet) at 31 December 2011			
	£000	£000	£000
NON-CURRENT ASSETS			
Freehold property at valuation		3,400	
Other non-current assets		8,256	
			11,656
CURRENT ASSETS	331		
Cash and cash equivalents	82		
		413	
Less CURRENT LIABILITIES		109	
Net current assets			304
			11,960
EQUITY			
Ordinary shares (8m)			**8,000**
Share premium			**0**
Revaluation reserve			**0**
Retained earnings			**3,960**
			11,960

Explanatory notes

1   The items in bold are those which are subject to change. In a bonus issue only the equity section of the statement of financial position (balance sheet) is affected.

2   The bonus issue adds 3.2m shares to the existing issued share capital of 4.8m shares of £1 each, so the value of ordinary shares at face value is £8m.

3   The share premium and revaluation reserve are used to finance the bonus issue (as their values are now both £0, they could, of course, left off the statement of financial position (balance sheet).

4 The retained earnings is the least affected by the bonus issue (so that dividend flexibility can be maintained): it is reduced by the £260 to complete the financing of the bonus issue.

Activity

The directors of each of the four companies below have decided to make a bonus issue of shares. In each case calculate the number of bonus shares that will be issued.

Company	Current issued capital	Face value of shares	Scale of bonus issue (number of bonus shares to number of existing shares)	Number of bonus shares
P plc	£12m	£1	1 for 4	
Q plc	£3.6m	25p	4 for 1	
R plc	£10m	50p	4 for 5	
S plc	£18m	£5	2 for 1	

Learning outcomes

As a result of studying this topic, you should now be able to:

■ explain the terms revaluation of non-current assets, rights issues of shares and bonus issues of shares

■ prepare a statement of changes in equity to show the effects of a revaluation of non-current assets, a rights issue of shares and a bonus issue of shares

■ evaluate rights issues by assessing the benefits and drawbacks of a rights issue of shares from the issuing company's viewpoint

■ evaluate bonus issues by assessing the benefits and drawbacks of a bonus issue from the issuing company's viewpoint and from a shareholder's viewpoint

AQA⁄ Examination Style Questions

1 The following trial balance was extracted from the books of DWK plc at 30 September 2011 immediately prior to the preparation of the company's statement of financial position (balance sheet) at that date.

	Dr £000	Cr £000
Current assets	114	
Current liabilities		93
Debentures (2019)		600

Freehold property	1,700	
Issued shares		1,200
Other non-current assets	960	
Retained earnings		431
Share premium		450
	2,774	2,774

The directors have decided to revalue the freehold property with immediate effect at £2,600,000.

Prepare the company's statement of financial position (balance sheet) at 30 September 2011 taking account of all the information.

2   The directors of Quextra plc have decided to make a rights issue of £1 ordinary shares. The company's summarised statement of financial position (balance sheet) immediately prior to the rights issue was as follows.

Summarised Statement of Financial Position (Balance Sheet) at 31 August 2011

	£000	£000
Non-current assets		4,770
Current assets	372	
less Current liabilities	111	
Net current assets		261
		5,031
Non-current (long-term) liabilities		800
		4,231
Equity		
Ordinary shares of £1 each		3,200
Share premium		420
Retained earnings		611
		4,231

Shareholders were offered 3 shares for every 4 currently held. The shares were offered at a premium of 70p each.

Prepare the company's summarised statement of financial position (balance sheet) immediately after the right issue. Assume the rights issue is fully subscribed.

3   The directors of Wrexford Ltd have decided to make a bonus issue of shares. The company's summarised statement of financial position (balance sheet) immediately prior to the bonus issue was as follows.

Summarised Statement of Financial Position (Balance Sheet) at 31 January 2012

	£000
Non-current assets	1,840
Net current assets	332
	2,172
Non-current liabilities	120
	2,052
Equity	
Ordinary shares of £1 each	600
Share premium	320
Revaluation reserve	540
Retained earnings	592
	2,052

Ordinary shareholders will receive 3 shares for every 2 shares currently held. The directors' policy is to maintain maximum flexibility in regard to the payment of cash dividends.

Prepare the company's summarised statement of financial position (balance sheet) at 31 January 2012 immediately after the bonus issue.

4   The directors of Xeraton plc decided to revalue the company's freehold land and buildings and to make a bonus issue of shares. Immediately prior to these events the company's summarised statement of financial position (balance sheet) was as follows.

Summarised Statement of Financial Position (Balance Sheet) at 30 November 2011

	£000	£000
Non-current assets		
Freehold land and buildings	3,200	
Other non-current assets	1,880	
		5,080
Current assets	331	
Less Current liabilities	176	
		155
		5,235
Non-current liabilities		500
		4,735
Equity		
Ordinary shares of 50p each		2,000
Share premium		800
Retained earnings		1,935
		4,735

The freehold property was revalued at £4,800,000 on 1 December 2011. The revaluation was followed on the same day by a bonus issue of 3 shares for every 2 shares currently held. The directors wished to maintain maximum flexibility in regard to the payment of cash dividends.

Prepare the company's summarised statement of financial position (balance sheet) at 1 December 2011 following the revaluation and bonus issue.

5   The directors of Aganza plc agreed to make a bonus issue of shares on 31 October 2011. The directors wished to retain the reserves in their most distributable form.

The equity section of the company's statement of financial position (balance sheet) immediately prior to the bonus issue was as follows:

EQUITY	£m
Authorised capital	
40m ordinary shares of 25p each	10
Issued capital	
10m ordinary shares of 25 p each	2.5
Share premium	1.3
Revaluation reserve	2.8
Retained earnings	3.9
	10.5

Shareholders were given 9 shares for every 5 shares currently held.

(a)   Prepare the equity section of the statement of financial position (balance sheet) after the bonus issue.

(b)   Explain why the directors might have chosen to make a bonus issue.

(c)   Assess the effect of the bonus issue on ordinary shareholders.

As you know, much hard work goes into preparing financial accounting records! All this effort would be largely wasted, however, if it was not used by interested parties, particularly owners and managers, to uncover how well or badly a business is performing. In this chapter you will learn some techniques for analysing business performance and learn how to judge just how well a business is doing. You will also be able to draw upon all your developing understanding of businesses to be able to suggest what should happen to further improve a business's performance. You will find that your skills in preparing the financial statements of sole traders and limited companies will now be of considerable value in understanding what these statements show about a business's financial health. You will principally be looking at a business's profitability and liquidity, but you will also consider how a company arranges its finance and why this could matter to the company and its shareholders. You will learn not only how to calculate 11 ratios, and gain an appreciation of why ratio analysis is useful but also why this process has its limitations. You will be learning how to write effective reports on business performance, in which you provide a careful evaluation of the business's financial strengths and weaknesses, based on ratio calculations and comparisons of the results with previous years or with other similar businesses.

1   Accounting ratios

In this topic you will learn:

- the names of, and formulae for, different ratios

- how to calculate each of the ratios

- how to explain why ratios are important

- how to explain the limitations of ratios

- how to explain the differences between cash and profit.

Case studies

Bayford Stores and Wexfield Ltd

Bayford Stores is located in the centre of Bayford. The business is owned by Indira Khan and it sells electrical goods. The business has been trading for a number of years.

Wexfield Ltd is a national chain of high-quality hotels. The company is financed by a mix of preference shares, ordinary shares and debentures.

The value of ratios

Why are ratios used to assess business performance?

Ratios provide a means of comparing the performance of a business

- from one year to the next
- with other similar businesses

They enable changes in important aspects of a business's performance to be pinpointed and quantified. The calculation of ratios enables trends to be highlighted.

The owners and managers of businesses will be eager to use ratios to assess performance. Other **stakeholders** will also be keen to assess performance and rivals will be interested, too. In the case of limited companies, potential investors will also take an interest.

Limitations of ratios

Are there any limitations to the use of ratios when measuring business performance?

Ratio analysis is of limited value because:

- it is applied to recent financial performance, in other words it is based on historical data, which may or may not have any direct relevance as to how the business will perform in the future
- it tends to use summarised accounting information (as shown in financial statements) and this information may hide a more complex story of partial successes offset by partial failures
- it can only be used with financial information, and so it cannot be used to assess other important factors about a business such as the qualities of the management team, the morale of employees, etc.
- statements of financial position (balance sheets) are for a particular moment in time and may not be entirely representative of how the business usually performs
- it relies on making comparisons of similar businesses, yet, however similar businesses may appear, there are bound to be important factors that make them different (for example the owner's or directors' mission for the business; differing accounting policies in regard to, say, provisions for doubtful debts)
- it uses elements in financial statements that may distort the picture (for example, the figure capital employed relies on totalling the values of assets, yet some of these – particularly property – may be undervalued on the statement of financial position (balance sheet))
- it cannot be used effectively for comparisons of businesses that are totally different in nature
- it relies on interpreting results and that is bound to be a subjective process.

Income statement ratios: part 1

Which ratios are used to analyse the trading section of an income statement and how are they calculated?

The three ratios used to analyse the trading section of an income statement are as follows:

Gross profit margin	$\dfrac{\text{Gross Profit}}{\text{Revenue}} \times 100$
Mark-up	$\dfrac{\text{Gross Profit}}{\text{Cost of sales}} \times 100$
Rate of inventory turnover	$\dfrac{\text{Cost of sales}}{\text{Average inventory}}$

Key terms

Gross profit margin: gross profit in relation to revenue (measured as a percentage).

Mark-up: gross profit in relation to cost of sales (measured as a percentage).

Rate of inventory turnover: cost of sales divided by average inventory.

Illustration

Calculating Bayford Stores's Income Statement Ratios

BAYFORD STORES
Income Statement for the year ended 31 December 2011 (Extract)

	£	£
Revenue		360,000
Less: Opening inventory	16,200	
Purchases	239,600	
	255,800	
Closing inventory	15,800	
		240,000
Gross profit		120,000

Figure 9.1 *Trading section*

Gross profit margin

$\dfrac{\text{Gross Profit}}{\text{Revenue}} \times 100$ i.e. $\dfrac{£120,000}{£360,000} \times 100$ i.e. 33.33%

Mark-up

$\dfrac{\text{Gross Profit}}{\text{Cost of sales}} \times 100$ i.e. $\dfrac{£120,000}{£240,000} \times 100$ i.e. 50%

Rate of inventory turnover

$\dfrac{\text{Cost of sales}}{\text{Average inventory}}$ i.e. $\dfrac{£240,000}{£16,000*}$ i.e. 15 times

* Average inventory was found by taking the average of the opening inventory (£16,200) and closing inventory (£15,800)

i.e. $\dfrac{£16,200 + £15,800}{2} = £16,000$

Background knowledge

The rate of inventory turnover is given as 'so many times' – i.e. in the example the average inventory was sold 15 times during the year. The formula to use if you wish to calculate the rate of inventory turnover in days is:

$\dfrac{\text{Average inventory}}{\text{Cost of sales}} \times 365$

Using the data in the example, the result would be 24 days. If both the opening and closing inventories are not available in the information provided, it is possible to use just the closing inventory in calculations rather than an average inventory figure.

Income statement ratios: part 2

Which ratios are used to analyse the profit and loss section of an income statement and how are they calculated?

The two ratios used to analyse the profit and loss section of an income statement are as follows:

Profit margin	$\dfrac{Profit}{Revenue} \times 100$
Overhead to turnover	$\dfrac{Overhead}{Revenue} \times 100$

Illustration

Calculating Bayford Stores's Income Statement Ratios

BAYFORD STORES
Income Statement for the year ended 31 December 2011 (Extract)

	£	£
Gross Profit		120,000
Less: administration expenses	12,000	
rent, rates and insurance	18,000	
wages and salaries	48,000	
depreciation of non-current asset	18,000	
		96,000
Profit		24,000

Figure 9.2 *Profit and loss section*

Profit margin

$\dfrac{Profit}{Revenue}$ × 100   i.e. $\dfrac{£24,000}{£360,000}$ × 100   i.e.   6.67%

Overhead/revenue

$\dfrac{Administration \ expenses}{Revenue}$ × 100   i.e. $\dfrac{£12,000}{£360,000}$ × 100   i.e.   3.33%

$\dfrac{Rent, \ rates \ and \ insurance}{Revenue}$ × 100   i.e. $\dfrac{£18,000}{£360,000}$ × 100   i.e.   5%

$\dfrac{Wages \ and \ salaries}{Revenue}$ × 100   i.e. $\dfrac{£48,000}{£360,000}$ × 100   i.e.   13.33%

$\dfrac{Depreciation}{Revenue}$ × 100   i.e. $\dfrac{£18,000}{£360,000}$ × 100   i.e.   5%

Statement of financial position (balance sheet) ratios

Which ratios are used to analyse a statement of financial position (balance sheet) and how are they calculated?

The six ratios used to analyse a statement of financial position (balance sheet) are as follows:

Return on capital employed	*For a sole trader:* $$\frac{\text{Profit}}{\text{Capital}} \times 100$$ Note: normally the opening capital is used for this ratio, but if this is not available it is possible to use the closing capital figure.
	For a limited company: $$\frac{\text{Profit before interest and tax}}{\textbf{Capital employed}} \times 100 \qquad i.e. \frac{\textit{Operating profit}}{\textit{Capital employed}} \times 100$$
Net current assets ratio (current ratio or working capital ratio)	Current assets : current liabilities
Liquid capital ratio (acid test ratio)	**Liquid capital** : current liabilities (liquid capital is current assets excluding inventories)
Receivable days	$$\frac{\text{Trade receivables}}{\text{Credit sales}} \times 365$$
Payable days	$$\frac{\text{Trade payables}}{\text{Credit purchases}} \times 365$$
Gearing	$$\frac{\text{Fixed return financing}}{\text{All sources of finance}} \times 100$$ *For a limited company:* $$\frac{\text{Preference shares + Non-current liabilities (e.g. debentures)}}{\text{Preference and Ordinary Shares + Reserves + Non-current liabilities}} \times 100$$

Table 9.1 *Six ratios used to analyse a statement of financial position (balance sheet)*

Activity

Sahera Ltd had a turnover of £20m in 2011. The company's gross profit for 2011 was £4.8 m; running costs for 2011 totalled £3.8 m. Calculate:

  a the business's profit
  b the percentage profit margin.

Activity

Ahmed & Co's turnover for a year was £1.5m and the business's cost of sales was £0.75m. Calculate

  a the gross profit and then state
  b the percentage mark-up and
  c the percentage gross profit margin.

Key terms

Return on capital employed: profit in relation to capital invested (sole trader) or capital employed (limited company), expressed as a percentage. This is an important measure of profitability.

Capital employed: for a limited company this is made up of shares + reserves + non-current liabilities.

Net current assets ratio: is current assets in relation to current liabilities; the ratio is sometimes called the current ratio or the working capital ratio. This is an important measure of liquidity.

Liquid capital: is current assets excluding inventories.

Activity

Kyle & Co's opening inventory on 1 January 2011 was £88,000; on 31 December the closing inventory was £72,000. During 2011 the business sold goods costing £960,000. Calculate:

a the average inventory for 2011

b the rate of inventory turnover for 2011 expressing your answer in days.

Background knowledge

Alternative formulas: there are a number of acceptable ways of measuring some ratios. For example, it is possible to use a sole trader's opening capital, closing capital, or an average of these when calculating a sole trader's return on capital invested. In the illustrations that follow, the opening capital has been used. There are a number of ways of measuring gearing. Again, any conventional formula would be accepted, but it is recommended that you use the formula given here.

Alternative names: some ratios have alternative names; any of the alternative names given here are accepted.

Illustration

Calculating Wexfield Ltd's statement of financial position (balance sheet) ratios

WEXFIELD Ltd
Statement of financial position (Balance Sheet) at 31 December 2011

	£	£	£
Non-current assets at net book value			1,530
Current assets			
Inventory	217		
Trade receivables	114		
Prepayments	5		
Cash and cash equivalents	44		
		380	
Current liabilities			
Trade payables	69		
Accruals	3		
Corporation tax	138		
		210	
Net current assets			170
			1,700
Non-current liabilities			
8% Debentures (2025)			(300)
			1,400
Equity			
1,600,000 ordinary shares of 50p each fully paid			800
200,000 7% preference shares of £1 each fully paid			200
Share premium			250
Retained earnings			150
			1,400

Figure 9.3 *Statement of financial position (balance sheet)*

Notes:

The company made an operating profit of £234,000 during the year ended 31 December 2011.

The company's total credit sales for the year ended 31 December 2011 were £1,400,000; credit purchases for the same period were £930,000.

Return on capital employed

$$\frac{\text{Profit before tax and interest}}{\text{Capital employed}} \times 100 \quad \text{i.e.} \quad \frac{£234,000}{£1,700,000} \times 100$$

i.e.   13.76%

Net current asset ratio/Current ratio/Working capital ratio

Current assets: current liabilities   i.e. £380,000: £210,000 i.e. 1.81:1

Liquid capital ratio/Acid test ratio

Liquid assets: current liabilities   i.e. £163,000: £210,000 i.e. 0.78:1

Receivable days

$$\frac{\text{Closing receivables}}{\text{Credit sales}} \times 365 \quad \text{i.e.} \quad \frac{£114,000}{£1,400,000} \times 365 \quad \text{i.e.} \quad 29.72 \text{ days} = 30 \text{ days}$$

Payable days

$$\frac{\text{Closing payables}}{\text{Credit purchases}} \times 365 \quad \text{i.e.} \quad \frac{£69,000}{£930,000} \times 365 \quad \text{i.e.} \quad 27.08 \text{ days} = 28 \text{ days}$$

Gearing

$$\frac{\text{Fixed return finance}}{\text{All sources of finance}} \times 100 \quad \text{i.e.} \quad \frac{£500,000}{£1,700,000} \times 100 \quad \text{i.e.} \quad 29.41\%$$

Fixed return finance is: preference share capital + debentures, i.e. £200,000 + £300,000, i.e. £500,000

All finance is: preference shares £200,000 + ordinary shares £800,000 + reserves £400,000 + debentures £300,000, i.e. £1,700,000

It is usual to express the receivable days and payable days ratio in whole days. Always round up – so 27.08 days has become 28 days.

Activity

Ortega & Co had total current assets of £140,000 including an inventory of £55,000, and current liabilities of £105,000 at 31 December 2011. Calculate:

a net current assets

b liquid assets

c net current assets ratio

d liquid capital ratio.

Cash versus profit

What are the differences between cash and profit?

Profits and cash are not necessarily the same for the following reasons.

Some accounting entries have an effect on profits but no effect on cash:

- depreciation of non-current assets
- provisions for doubtful debts

Some accounting entries have an effect on cash but no effect on the calculation of net profit:

- purchasing non-current assets
- borrowing money (including debentures in the case of a limited company)
- repaying loans (including debentures in the case of a limited company)
- owner's drawings (or dividends in the case of limited companies)

AQA Examiner's tip

Always state the formula you are using.

Background knowledge

The net current assets ratio and liquid capital ratio should always be expressed as xx:1.

Background knowledge

The liquid capital (acid test) ratio excludes inventory, this is because it is assumed that this is the least liquid of a business's current assets, i.e. inventories take the longest time to be turned into cash.

Activity

Phil Wentworth's business had credit sales totalling £328,500 during its most recently completed financial year. At the year-end trade receivables totalled £27,000. Calculate the receivable days.

Activity

Sarah Ratcliffe Ltd is financed by debentures £500,000 and shareholders' funds of £1,500,000. The company does not have any preference shares. Calculate the company's gearing ratio.

■ Activity

Croxley Wholesale Ltd recently made annual profits of £400,000 but completed the year with a bank overdraft of £30,000. Identify **four** different types of transaction that might account for this situation.

■ Background knowledge

Sometimes the owners or managers of a business may think that, because their business has made a profit, there should be a substantial cash balance at the year end and may be puzzled if the bank balance is an overdraft. The reverse can also apply: a business can be operating at a loss yet have a satisfactory bank balance.

- additional capital introduced by the owner (or the issue of shares in the case of limited companies)
- payment of tax

Some other transactions have an immediate effect on profits but a delayed effect on cash:

- credit sales
- credit purchases
- expense accruals

Some other transactions have an immediate effect on cash but a delayed effect on profit:

- unsold inventory
- prepayments
- purchase of a non-current asset (leading to depreciation of the non-current asset)

Learning outcomes

As a result of studying this topic, you should now be able to:

■ identify, state the formula for, and calculate the following ratios: gross profit margin, mark up, rate of inventory turnover, profit margin, expense to revenue, return on capital employed, net current assets (working capital) ratio, liquid capital (acid test) ratio, receivable days, creditor payable days, gearing

■ explain why ratios are important

■ explain the limitations of ratios

■ explain the differences between cash and profit

AQA↗ Examination Style Questions

1   Ian Wong, a wholesaler, presented the following final accounts for his business at the end of its most recently completed financial year.

Income Statement for the year ended 31 October 2011	£000	£000
Revenue		1,880
Less Opening inventory	27	
Purchases	1,416	
	1,443	
Closing inventory	33	
Cost of sales		1,410
Gross profit		470
Administration expenses	235	
Selling and distribution expenses	94	
		329
Profit for the year		141

Calculate the following ratios

■ gross profit margin %
■ mark-up %
■ rate of inventory turnover
■ profit margin
■ administration expenses/revenue %
■ selling and distributions expenses/revenue %

2   MZQ Ltd's financial year ended on 31 January 2012. Its statement of financial position (balance sheet) on that date was as follows.

Statement of financial position (Balance Sheet) at 31 January 2012	£000	£000	£000
NON-CURRENT ASSETS			1,650
CURRENT ASSETS			
Inventory	172		
Receivables	56		
Cash and cash equivalents	37		
		265	
CURRENT LIABILITIES			
Payables	44		
Corporation tax due	51		
		95	
Net current assets			170
			1820
NON-CURRENT LIABILITIES			
7% Debentures (2021)			500
			1320
EQUITY			
Ordinary shares of £1 each			700
8% Preference shares of £1 each			200
Share premium			140
Retained earnings			280
			1320

Additional information

1   The company's profit before interest for the year ended 31 January 2012 was £209,000.
2   For the year ended 31 January 2012, the company's credit purchases totalled £472,353 and credit sales totalled £567,777.

Calculate the following ratios:

■ return on capital employed %
■ net current assets ratio
■ liquid capital ratio
■ receivable days (receivables collection period)
■ payable days (creditor payment period)
■ gearing %

3   The managing director of Eleford Ltd is surprised to learn that the company has a positive bank balance despite having made a loss for the year under review.
     (a)   Explain why a business's profit and cash funds can be out of step with each other.
     (b)   Provide **three** possible reasons for the situation reported by the managing director of Eleford Ltd

2   Assessing business performance

In this topic you will learn:

■ how to explain what each of the ratios can tell you about a business

■ to prepare a report on a business's performance

■ to identify appropriate ratios to be used in the assessment

■ how to calculate these ratios

■ to analyse ratios to reveal what they mean in terms of the business's performance

■ how to make a judgement about the strengths and weaknesses of the business's performance

■ how to make recommendations that will enable the business's performance to improve.

■ Gross profit margin and mark-up

What does the gross profit margin and mark-up percentages tell you about a business's performance?

Gross profit margin percentage tells you:

■ how much gross profit is being made in relation to revenue (in end of year financial statements)

■ how much gross profit (in pence) is being made for every £1 of revenue (in end of year financial statements).

Mark-up percentage is very similar but tells you:

■ how much gross profit is being made in relation to the cost of sales

■ for each £1 of cost of sales how much gross profit (in pence) is being made

and (for both ratios) if the percentage is increasing:

■ either that the business has changed its pricing policy and has put selling prices up

■ or that the business is paying less for the goods it sells

and (for both ratios) if the percentage is decreasing:

■ either that the business has changed its pricing policy and has put selling prices down

■ or that the business is paying more for the goods its sells.

Further means of interpreting these ratios:

There could be a variety of factors behind changes in these ratios: changes in trends or inventory control or market supply, for example.

If you know the typical gross profit margin or mark up percentages for a particular type of business you can comment on whether:

■ the business's selling price policy is too high or too low

■ the business is paying too much or too little for the goods it purchases.

■ Rate of inventory turnover

What does the rate of inventory turnover tell you about a business's performance?

The rate of inventory turnover:

■ compares the average inventory to the total cost of inventory sold during a period

■ it indicates how quickly inventories are being sold.

If the rate is increasing:

■ perhaps the business is selling more inventory

■ or perhaps the average inventory held is being reduced.

If the rate is decreasing:

- perhaps the business is selling less inventory
- or perhaps the business is holding more average inventory.

For a business to see the rate of inventory turnover increasing because it is selling more goods would, of itself, be an encouraging sign. The more revenue the more chance to earn a gross profit. However, one would need to bear in mind why more inventories were being sold before making a final judgment. Perhaps there has been increased revenue because of price cuts, for example, but if the price cut was too severe there could be a negative impact on gross profit.

For a business to see a change in the rate of inventory turnover because average inventory is changing could be interpreted in a variety of ways. To reduce average inventories could be a good move because the business could reduce its storage costs. On the other hand, if it goes too far with this, the choice available to customers may be reduced and this could impact on revenue.

Further means of interpreting this ratio

If you know the typical rate of inventory turnover for a type of business you can comment on whether a business's result is higher or lower and suggest why this might be happening. For example, if the rate of inventory turnover is too low, you could suggest that possibly the business is charging too much for the goods it sells, which is depressing revenue, or that it is holding too much average inventory.

Profit margin and overheads/revenue ratios

What does the profit margin and overheads/revenue percentages tell you about a business's performance?

The **profit margin** percentage tells you:

- how much profit is being made in relation to revenue
- how much profit (in pence) is being made for every £1 of revenue.

If the percentage is increasing, this tells you that:

- either the business is making more gross profit
- or that costs have been held at previous level or reduced
- or some combination of these factors.

If the percentage is decreasing, this tells you that:

- either the business is making less gross profit
- or that costs have risen above previous levels
- or some combination of these factors.

The **overheads/revenue** percentage tells you:

- how much is being spent on an overhead in relation to revenue
- for each £1 of revenue how much (in pence) is being paid for an overhead.

If the percentage is increasing, this tells you that:

- the business is less efficient than it was previously in regard to controlling costs.

If the percentage is decreasing, this tells you that:

- the business is more efficient than it was previously in regard to controlling costs.

AQA Examiner's tip

When comparing ratios make sure the data has been presented in the same form. For example, you cannot directly compare a rate of inventory turnover of six times with a rate of 28 days.

AQA Examiner's tip

Approach data in a simple way to start with, for example:

- what's happened to revenue (all businesses like to see this increasing as it is often the key to success)
- what has happened to the ratios: are they increasing or decreasing, or is the picture more mixed?
- is the pattern of change in the ratios a good thing or a bad thing for the business?

Then try to see if you can deduce any important information from the data that can help you make a judgement about the business's success. For example, in the illustration it is possible to work out that gross profit has been improving over the three-year period.

Then try to explain what may have caused the changes in the ratio.

Finally, have a clear view as to whether the business's overall performance is improving or not.

Background knowledge

The average figures for a type of business are sometimes called 'benchmarking data', 'industrial averages' or 'sector averages'.

Further means of interpreting these ratios

If you know the benchmark figures for a type of business, you can comment on whether the business is operating more efficiently or less efficiently than is usual.

> ### ■ Activity
>
> Desdra Stores has improved its gross profit margin for its most recently completed financial year, but it has not made any changes to its pricing policy. At the same time, the rate of inventory turnover has fallen. Furthermore, the profit margin has declined. Identify one reason for:
>
> **a** the improvement in the gross profit margin
>
> **b** the fall in the rate of inventory turnover
>
> **c** the decline in the profit margin.

■ Return on capital employed

What does the return on capital employed percentage tell you about a business's performance?

The **return on capital employed** percentage measures:

- profit in relation to capital employed
- how much profit (in pence) is made for every £1 of capital employed.

If the return on capital employed percentage is increasing it tells you:

- either the business is making more profit
- or the business has employed less capital
- or some combination of both these factors
- that the business is using its resources (in the form of assets) more effectively.

If the return on capital employed percentage is decreasing it tells you:

- either the business is making less profit
- or the business has employed more capital
- or some combination of both these factors
- that the business is using its resources less effectively.

Further means of interpreting these ratios

A business's return on capital employed could be compared to the return for similar businesses if these benchmark figures are available. In the case of a sole trader, if might be possible to consider how well the sole trader would do if the capital tied up in the business was invested, and if the sole trader, instead, was in employment earning a salary. In making such a comparison, it would be important to remember how relatively risky it is to invest in a business compared to investing in a savings account.

■ Net current assets and liquid capital ratios

What do the net current assets and liquid capital ratios tell you about a business's performance?

The **net current assets ratio** measures:

- current assets in relation to current liabilities
- the amount of current assets available to pay the short-term 'debts' of the business.

The **liquid capital ratio** is similar because it measures:

■ liquid assets in relation to current liabilities

■ the amount of liquid assets available to pay 'the debts' of the business.

The difference between the ratios is one of timing. Net current assets looks at liquidity and cash flow issues further ahead than liquid capital. Liquid capital is a more immediate measure of liquidity (hence the term 'acid test ratio').

If the two ratios are *increasing*:

■ this could imply that the business will find it easier to pay its debts (a strength)

■ or that it has too many resources tied up as current assets or liquid capital (a weakness).

If the two ratios are *decreasing*:

■ this could imply that the business will find it more difficult to pay its debts (a weakness)

■ or that it has reduced the resources tied up as current assets or liquid capital to a more efficient level (a strength).

Whether the change in the ratios should be interpreted as a strength or a weakness depends on the benchmark figures for the type of business concerned. These benchmarks vary considerably. For example, supermarket chains needs relatively low ratios in order to operate effectively, because their sales are overwhelmingly in cash and they tend to have a high rate of inventory turnover for most of their products. Contrast this with, say, a furniture store, where there is likely to be a relatively high level of credit sales and relatively low rates of inventory turnover.

Activity

Orbell Ltd's profit has decreased considerably since last year, but its return on capital employed has improved. At the same time the business's liquid capital ratio has increased. Explain one reason why

a the return on capital employed has improved

b the liquid capital ratio has increased

c the increase in the liquid capital ratio may be bad news for the business.

Receivable days and payable days

What do the receivable days and payable days ratios tell you about a business's performance?

The **receivable days ratio** measures:

■ how many days on average a credit customer takes to pay.

If the receivable days ratio is *increasing* this tells you that receivables are taking longer to pay than previously.

This change can be interpreted as being:

■ a weakness because it could imply that credit control is not being as carefully managed as previously and this could lead to an increase in bad debts

Background knowledge

Short-term 'debts' of the business would include all the items on which the business will need to use cash resources in the near future. These should include the current liabilities, such as trade payables, but may also include:

■ many expenses (because these tend to be paid at frequent intervals)

■ loan repayments

■ the owner's drawings (or dividend payments for a limited company)

■ planned purchases of non-current assets

■ payments of tax.

AQA Examiner's tip

Avoid generalising about the correct net current assets ratio or liquid capital ratio for businesses to have. Some candidates write about an ideal ratio. This is to be avoided, because the appropriate ratio depends very much on the type of business. For example, compare supermarkets and furniture stores as illustrated in the main text.

Key terms

Receivable days: trade receivables in relation to credit sales; the ratio is expressed as so many days.

■ a strength if previously credit control was too tight, and the change has resulted in a greater volume of credit sales.

If the receivable days ratio is *decreasing* this tells you that receivables are taking a shorter time to pay than previously.

This change can be interpreted as being:

■ a strength because it could imply that credit control is being more carefully managed than previously and this could reduce the amount of bad debts

■ a weakness if previously credit control was about right, and the change has resulted in a decline in credit sales because rival businesses offer better credit terms.

The **payable days ratio** measures:

■ how many days are taken on average to pay for credit purchases.

If the payable days ratio is *increasing* this tells you that a business is taking longer to pay its payables than previously.

This change can be interpreted as being:

■ a weakness because it could mean that the business is exceeding the credit period allowed by suppliers and as a result suppliers may discontinue offering credit facilities

■ a strength as cash flow will be improved.

If the payable days ratio is *decreasing* this tells you that the business is taking less time to pay payables.

This change can be interpreted as being:

■ a strength because it could imply that credit control is being more carefully managed and that difficulties with suppliers exceeding credit limits will no longer occur

■ a weakness if the business is now paying suppliers earlier than necessary, resulting in a negative impact on cash flow.

Further means of interpreting these ratios

It is useful to compare the receivable days ratio with the payable days ratio. If the payable days ratio is shorter than the receivable days ratio this will have a negative impact on cash flow. If the situation is reversed, i.e. receivables pay more quickly than the business pays suppliers, this will have a positive impact on cash flow. The latter is recommended for long-term cash management control.

■ **Illustration**

Assessing the performance of Bayford Stores

The following ratios have been calculated for Bayford Stores for the years 2010 and 2011.

	2010	2011
Gross profit margin	35%	33.3%
Mark-up	53.8%	50%
Rate of stock turnover	12 times	14 times
Profit margin	16%	18%

Wages and salaries to revenue	34%	37%
Return on capital employed	18%	17%
Net current assets ratio	2.3 : 1	1.9 : 1
Liquid capital ratio	1.5 : 1	1.4 : 1
Receivable days	36 days	31 days
Payable days	33 days	34 days

Table 9.2 *Calculated ratios*

Additional information:

Revenue was £310,000 in 2010 and £340,000 in 2011

Benchmarks for this business sector:

■ Net current assets ratio 1.8:1
■ Liquid capital ratio 1.4:1

Assess the performance of Bayford Stores comparing 2011 with 2010

Strengths

Revenue has increased substantially between the two years (by £30,000). This could be due to the reduction in the gross profit margin (by 1.7%) and mark-up percentages (by 3.8%) which may imply that selling prices have been reduced giving the business a more competitive edge.

The rate of inventory turnover has increased (from 12 to 14 times a year). This could have resulted from the increase in revenue between the two years; it might also be due to a reduction in average inventory perhaps saving storage costs.

The profit margin percentage has increased (by 2%). This may just have resulted from the increased revenue, but could also have resulted from some efficiencies in controlling expenses.

Both liquidity ratios have fallen slightly and are now nearer (in the case of the net current assets ratio) or exactly in line with (in the case of the liquid capital ratio) the sector averages. This suggests that liquid resources are being managed more efficiently.

The receivable days have decreased (by 5 days) implying greater credit control. At the same time the payable days have lengthened (by 1 day) which may have helped conserve the business's liquid resources. Whereas payables were being paid more frequently than amounts due from receivables were being collected, this position has now been reversed.

Weaknesses

Despite the improvement in the profit percentage, wages and salaries have increased (by 3%) out of proportion to the increase in sales. This could imply that this cost has not been so effectively controlled.

The return on capital employed has fallen (by 1%) despite increased profits. The implication is that there has been an increase in capital invested in the company and that capital is now earning slightly less profits than previously, so resources are not being used as effectively as before.

AQA Examiner's tip

There are various approaches to take if a question like this comes up in your exam. The merit of the answer provided is that:

■ there is a clear statement about whether a ratio has increased or decreased and by how much.

■ some development in the form of an explanation as to what may lie behind the change in the ratio.

■ clear judgements (strengths, weaknesses)

■ a final overall judgement and a recommendation.

Final judgement and recommendation

Overall the business's performance has improved since 2010 with increased revenue, profits and more efficient liquidity ratios. However, the owner should address the slight decline in one key ratio, i.e. the return on capital employed.

Gearing

What does the gearing ratio tell you about a limited company's performance?

The **gearing ratio** measures:

- how a company is financed
- finance on which there is a fixed return compared to all of a company's finance.

If the percentage is *above 50%*, this tells you that the company:

- is high-geared
- has high amounts of fixed-return financing in relation to all financing
- will be able to pay interest/dividends on the fixed-return financing reasonably easily if the company is doing well in terms of profits
- may have difficulty in meeting its commitment to pay interest/dividends if the company is not doing well and profits are low, or a loss is being made
- may find it difficult to borrow more, because it already has a relatively high amount of fixed-return finance.

If the percentage is *below 50%*, this tells you that the company:

- is low-geared
- has low amounts of fixed-return financing in relation to all financing
- will tend to experience very few problems in meeting commitments to pay interest/dividends
- may find it relatively easy to borrow additional funds, because it currently has low levels of borrowing.

Further means of interpreting the gearing ratio

High-geared companies are often referred to as high-risk companies; conversely low-geared companies are often referred to as low-risk companies. The risk element refers to the company's vulnerability if profits are low or non-existent.

Stakeholders will be interested in the gearing ratio for a variety of reasons. For example, an ordinary shareholder will be concerned about the impact on profits, and therefore dividend payments, if a company becomes high-geared.

▨ Illustration

Assessing Benetex plc's gearing ratio

Benetex plc's gearing ratios over a three-year period were as follows:

	Year 1	Year 2	Year 3
Gearing	70%	50%	30%

Table 9.3 *Gearing ratios*

Basic observation:

▨ the gearing percentage has fallen over the 3-year period

▨ the company has moved from being high-geared to low-geared.

Interpretation:

The reduction in the gearing ratio means that the company has reduced its financing from debentures or other long-term loans and/or from preference shares. Alternatively, the reduction in the ratio could be due to increased financing from ordinary shares and/or building up reserves. The company will now be less vulnerable if profits fall because it has a lower proportion of fixed-return finance than previously. The company will find it is in a better position to borrow funds if this is necessary. The decline in the gearing ratio means the company has moved from being a high-risk to a low-risk company.

Learning outcomes

As a result of studying this topic, you should now be able to:

▨ prepare a report on the financial performance of a sole trader or a limited company with a focus on profitability and liquidity

▨ analyse the performance of a business comparing results over a period of years

▨ assess the performance of a business comparing it with other similar businesses or with benchmarks for businesses in the same sector

▨ evaluate a business's performance by assessing strengths and weaknesses in performance

▨ make recommendations as to how a business's performance could be improved

AQA↗ Examination Style Questions

1   The following ratios have been calculated as a result of analysing the end of year financial statements of the retail business owned by Vicky Chambers.

	For year ended 28 February		
	2009	**2010**	**2011**
Gross profit margin	20%	23%	26%
Mark up	25%	30%	35%
Rate of inventory turnover	21 times	23 times	24 times
Profit margin	9%	10%	12%
Salaries/revenue	7%	6%	5%
General expenses/revenue	4%	5%	6%

Revenue figures for each of these years are as follows:

2009   £1,300,000
2010   £1,450,000
2011   £1,530,000

Comment on the trend in the business's performance during the three-year period. For each ratio:
■ describe the trend and state whether this is a strength or a weakness
■ explain what may have caused the change.

2   Andy Kin has been looking at his business's end of year financial statements for each of the years ended 31 January 2010 and 2011. He has worked out the following accounting ratios based on these statements.

	2010	2011
Gross profit margin	29%	27%
Mark up	41%	37%
Profit/revenue	14%	10%
Operating expenses/revenue	13%	13%
Return on capital employed	13%	15%
Working capital ratio	1.2:1	1.5:1
Liquid capital ratio	0.8:1	0.7:1
Rate of inventory turnover	11 times	10 times
Receivable days	38 days	31 days
Payable days	37 days	30 days

The following information is available about revenue in each of the years ended 31 January:

2010   £680,000
2011   £730,000

Typical liquidity ratios for this type of business are:

working capital $\quad$ 1:4:1
liquid capital $\qquad$ 0.7:1

Prepare a report on this business's performance.

3 $\quad$ An analysis of the statements of financial position (balance sheets) of Meretrix Ltd at 31 December 2009, 2010 and 2011 produced the following ratios.

Statement of financial position (Balance Sheet) at 31 December			
	2009	**2010**	**2011**
Return on capital employed	19%	17%	15%
Net current assets ratio	2.7:1	2.4:1	2.3:1
Liquid capital ratio	1.8:1	1.7:1	1.4:1
Receivable days	31 days	33 days	35 days
Payable days	35 days	32 days	30 days
Gearing	63%	49%	41%

Additional information

Benchmarking figures for other companies in this sector show that average net current assets ratio are typically 2:3:1 and liquid capital ratios typically 1.6:1.

Comment on the company's performance over the three-year period. For each ratio (i) describe the trend and assess whether this is a strength or a weakness; (ii) explain what may have caused the changes over the three-year period.

4 $\quad$ The following extracts have been taken from the statements of financial position (balance sheets) of Priorford Ltd at 31 December 2010 and 2011.

Statement of financial position (Balance Sheet) (extracts) at 31 December		
	2010	**2011**
	£000	**£000**
NON-CURRENT (long-term) LIABILITIES		
10% Debentures	800	1,600
EQUITY		
Ordinary shares of 50p each	2,400	2,900
6% Preferences Shares of £1 each	800	1,600
Revaluation reserve	–	200
Share premium	400	500
Retained earnings	800	700
	4,400	5,900

(a) $\quad$ Calculate the gearing ratio at 31 December 2010 and 2011. State the formula used.

(b) $\quad$ Comment on the change in the gearing ratio and explain its significance for the ordinary shareholders of the company.

5   The following ratios have been calculated for three retail businesses operating in the same sector. The ratios are based on the annual accounts of each of these companies for the year ended 31 October 2011.

	Areton Ltd	Borford Ltd	Cragbury Ltd
Gross profit margin	45%	47%	46%
Profit margin	19%	20%	22%
Return on capital employed	17%	16%	18%

Benchmarking information for this retail sector is as follows:

Gross profit margin	46%
Profit margin	23%
Return on capital employed	17%

Comment on the relative performance of each of these three companies taking account of the benchmarking data.

10 Introduction to budgeting and budgetary control

So far all your work in accounting has been about recording financial information about past events. However, accounting techniques can also be useful in preparing forecasts of the future for individual businesses, so that owners and managers can make much more informed and effective decisions to improve their business's performance. You will develop an understanding of the advantages that businesses can gain from preparing budgets, but also develop an awareness of the limitations of this procedure. In this chapter you will learn how budgeting techniques can be used to predict future cash balances by producing cash budgets. Your existing knowledge of cash transactions will help you understand how businesses receive and spend money. Your understanding of credit transactions will help you understand why there will be a delay in receiving cash from receivables and a delay in making payments to payables. Your understanding of depreciation will also be useful, because you will be quick to realise that depreciation has no effect on a business's cash resources.

Case study

Bookworm

Bookworm is owed by Katy Thomas. It is a small second-hand bookshop that Katy opened in January 2010 and it is located in a small market town. Katy is a great book lover and she has a real flair for getting customers interested in her second-hand books. However, she has relatively little financial knowledge or experience.

Link

For more information on budgets, see *A2 Accounting*, Unit 4.

The advantages of budgeting

Why businesses prepare budgets: the advantages of budgeting

■ Budgets ensure that business activity has been carefully *planned* by the owners or managers.

■ They also provide a basis for *monitoring* actual activity against forecasts.

■ They enable expenditure to be *controlled* more effectively.

■ Budgets ensure that business activity is *co-ordinated*.

Illustration

The benefits Katy will gain from preparing budgets for Bookworm

When Katy started the business she approached her bank for a loan. She was required to prepare a cash budget in support of her loan application. This was a condition of lending Katy some of the funds she needed to get the business started.

Planning: In order to prepare her cash budget, Katy had to carefully consider what her business objectives should be. She started by thinking about how much drawings she would need to take out of the business each month in order to finance her living expenses. She also worked out how much she would have to pay in business rent, rates, insurance and other expenses. Next she considered how much she was likely to pay for inventories of second-hand books and the levels of mark-up that would attract, rather than deter, customers. As a result of these considerations, she was able to set targets for monthly sales. She had to work through these plans several times over to ensure that she would be able to meet her objectives with realistic figures.

Monitoring: having planned levels of sales and expenditure of running costs, inventories and drawings, Katy was in position to prepare a detailed cash budget. As she began trading, she was able to compare actual sales figures, and actual expenditure, with her detailed plan. She found this every useful, because she was able to quickly spot when actual events were different from her forecasts. For example, in June 2010 she noted that sales were much higher than predicted. She investigated why this was so and found that she had not realised an annual festival would be taking place in the town centre where Bookworm was located, and this brought in many tourists who visited the bookshop. As a result of this careful comparison she was able to adjust her budget for future years to take account of the June festival. In other words, Katy carefully monitored actual events against forecasts and where they did not match up, she took the trouble to investigate the reasons.

Control: Katy's carefully planned cash budget set limits to how much she could spend each month on running costs and inventories. For example, her cash budget showed clearly that she could afford to spend £3,500 on new inventories in September 2010. This amount of expenditure would be sufficient to keep the bookshop well stocked without causing the bank account to be overdrawn. In other words, the cash budget, in setting limits for each type of expenditure, controlled her spending.

Co-ordination: Katy's carefully prepared cash budget resulted not just from careful planning, but also giving some thought to the timing of various events. For example, Katy quickly came to realise that if she was to base her plans on realistic levels of sales and build in to the budget the required amount of drawings, she would not be able to furnish and equip her business as thoroughly as she would like in the early years. In other words, she had to bring together all the factors involved in establishing a successful business in her cash budget and this required some careful scheduling of events. Her budget was, therefore, carefully co-ordinated.

Further benefits of budgeting

In large organisations, budgeting often involves many of the employees in the planning stages. Where this is done effectively, *staff motivation* often increases. Staff feel they have had a part to play in setting the targets that they are to reach and, as a result, become more determined to reach these targets.

Budgets are also an effective means of *communicating* targets throughout an organisation from managers to staff. Where there is a comprehensive budgeting system in place, individuals are able to identify how their work for a part of the organisation fits in with the whole.

■ Disadvantages of budgeting

What are the potential disadvantages of budgeting?

■ Budgets can act as strait-jackets and as a result important but unexpected opportunities can be turned down.

■ Budgets can de-motivate staff if the targets set are too challenging of if the staff feel the targets have been imposed upon them.

■ On the other hand, budgets may be rather undemanding, so that targets set can be easily reached and the business's potential not fully realised.

■ Illustration

The possible drawbacks of preparing budgets for Bookworm

Katy's cash budget for November 2010 showed that she could afford to spend £4,100 on second-hand books. In early November she attended a monthly book auction. At the auction a rare opportunity arose to acquire a considerable number of second-hand books being sold off really cheaply by the owner of a large country house for £9,000. Katy, however, kept to her budget limit of £4,100. Katy was probably wrong to feel constrained by her budget, because she could have acquired valuable inventories at a low price. Maybe she would have been overdrawn at the bank, but in the longer term she might have a good profit on the additional inventories purchased at a good price.

■ Activity

Matt Bennett has decided that it could be a good idea for a cash budget to be prepared. Identify:

a   four benefits that could arise from preparing a cash budget

b   two drawbacks that could arise from preparing a cash budget.

Preparing cash budgets

How do businesses prepare cash budgets?

Cash budgets are usually prepared on a month-by-month basis. The main elements in the budget are:

■ *forecast opening balance* for the first month in the budget period

■ *forecast opening balances* for the second and subsequent months in the budget period (these balances will result from carrying forward the closing balance from the previous month)

■ *forecast receipts* from cash sales, from receivables paying for credit sales relating to the previous month or months, additional borrowing, additional capital investment, interest and/or rent received, cash received from the sale of non-current assets

■ *forecast payments* for purchases, to payables paying for the purchases relating to the previous month or months, for expenses, drawings (or dividend payments), loan repayments, purchases of non-current assets, etc.

■ *closing balances* for each month to be calculated as follows: opening balance + receipts for the month – payments for the month.

The figures to be entered will result from the setting of carefully thought out objectives and planning of future activities.

One of the main points of preparing a cash budget is to establish what the closing cash balance will be each month, based on the owner's or management's plans. If the cash budget reveals that there will a shortage of cash in any particular month, then suitable action can be taken to ensure the funds will be available to cover the shortage (for example, by arranging a bank overdraft) or by adjusting the plans to avoid the shortage (for example, postponing the purchase of a non-current asset). On the

■ Key terms

Cash budget: a plan showing estimated future receipts and payments that enables possible surpluses or shortages of cash to be identified.

Background knowledge

Budgets could be prepared for different time spans other than monthly. For example, a business could decide to break the budget down into three-monthly periods.

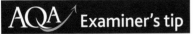

Examiner's tip

A common mistake is to include non-cash items in a cash budget, the most obvious example of which is depreciation.

Activity

A business's budget period begins with a balance at bank of £3,000. Total receipts for month 1 are £12,500 and total payments for month 1 are £17,200. Total receipts for month 2 are £13,600 and total payments for month 2 are £8,700. Calculate the closing bank balance for

a   month 1

b   month 2.

other hand, if there is surplus cash in any month, action can be taken to ensure that the surplus is invested to provide interest, or the budget plans are adjusted to make better use of cash resources in some other way. A final version of the cash budget will be useful evidence of careful management and expertise, should the owner wish to apply for a bank loan. It will also provide evidence that the business can afford to make monthly interest payments and, of course, repay the loan.

Illustration

Preparing a cash budget for Bookworm

Katy Thomas has ambitious plans for Bookworm for the four-month period ending 31 December 2011. She will continue to purchase some stock for cash, but has also arranged credit terms with a new supplier of second-hand books. She has also agreed to offer credit terms to a few of her more important customers.

Her detailed plans are as follows:

1   Cash balances on 1 September 2011 are expected to be £3,800.

2   Total monthly sales for the 5-month period August to December 2011 are forecast to be:

	£
August	5,000
September	5,400
October	5,600
November	4,800
December	6,400

Eighty per cent of all sales will be for cash. Remaining sales will be on credit terms.

Katy Thomas plans to offer one month's credit.

3   Cash purchases during the budget period are planned to be:

	£
September	1,600
October	1,100
November	3,200
December	2,600

4   The new supplier of second-hand books has offered her two months' credit and this arrangement is due to begin in September 2011. Katy plans to make the following credit purchases from this supplier:

	£
September	800
October	1,200
November	1,300
December	900

5   Katy has arranged with her landlord to pay rent of £800 per month quarterly in advance. Payments are due on 1 February, 1 May, etc.

6   Other expenses payments are forecast as follows:

	£
September	600
October	700
November	1,000
December	1,400

7 Katy plans to have monthly cash drawings of £2,200.

8 Katy will repay the bank loan at the rate of £300 per month. The last instalment is due in November 2011.

BOOKWORM CASH BUDGET

for each of the 4 months ending 31 December 2011

	September	October	November	December
	£	£	£	£
RECEIPTS				
Cash sales	4,320	4,480	3,840	5,120
Credit sales	1,000	1,080	1,120	960
	5,320	5,560	4,960	6,080
Cash purchases	1,600	1,100	3,200	2,600
Credit purchases			800	1,200
Rent			2,400	
Other expenses	600	700	1,000	1,400
Drawings	2,200	2,200	2,200	2,200
Loan repayment	300	300	300	
	4,700	4,300	9,900	7,400
Opening balance	3,800	4,420	5,680	740
Total receipts	5,320	5,560	4,960	6,080
	9,120	9,980	10,640	6,820
Less Total payments	4,700	4,300	9,900	7,400
Closing balance	4,420	5,680	740	−580

Figure 10.1 *Cash budget*

AQA Examiner's tip

Timing of receipts and payments: whereas cash sales and cash purchases can be entered in a cash budget with relative ease, receipts from receivables and payments to payables will need a more cautious approach, for example:

■ if payables allow one month's credit, the entry for payables in the cash budget for a particular month will relate to the credit purchases made in the previous month

■ if receivables are allowed two months' credit, the entry for receivables in the cash budget for a particular month will relate to credit sales made two months previously.

■ **Background knowledge**

Many private individuals prepare budgets. For example, students in higher education, aware that finances are likely to be difficult and that there could be a real anxiety about building up substantial debts, are often advised to prepare cash budgets. There is the possibility of gaining all the advantages listed above from this activity if it is undertaken with care, but, of course, some of the disadvantages could arise, too.

Learning outcomes

As a result of studying this chapter, you should now be able to:

■ explain why businesses prepare budgets

■ evaluate budgeting by considering the possible advantages and disadvantages of this process

■ prepare cash budgets

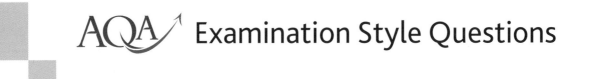

AQA Examination Style Questions

1   Seema Pulchan intends to set up a business which will start trading on 1 January 2013. Her bank has asked to a cash budget for the first four months the business is in operation. Seema's initial plans are as follows.

   (a)   She will introduce capital of £60,000 which will be paid into the business's bank account on 1 January 2013. On the same day the bank will make available a loan of £25,000.

   (b)   Sales (all cash) are expected to be as follows:

	£
January	15,300
February	16,200
March	18,100
April	21,400

   (c)   Purchases will be as follows:

	£
January	12,600
February	10,200
March	10,600
April	11,000

   Some suppliers are prepared to offer Seema one month's credit. Seema estimates that 20% of purchases will be on a cash basis; 80% of purchases will be made on one month's credit.

   (d)   Expense payments will be as follows:

	£
January	1,100
February	700
March	900
April	16,000

   (e)   Seema estimates she will need to withdraw £2,750 per month for her personal living expenses.

   (f)   The bank will require loan repayments of £1,800 per month starting in February 2013.

   (g)   Capital expenditure will amount to £55,000, of which £25,000 will be paid in January 2013, followed by three monthly payments of £10,000 per month.

   Prepare the cash budget for Seema Pulchan's business for each of the 4 months ending 30 April 2013.

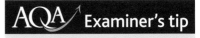

AQA Examiner's tip

Layout of cash budgets: there are a variety of ways of setting out a cash budget. All conventional layouts are accepted. You are advised to get used to using more than one layout, as the examination question may provide a particular template for your answer.

2   The directors of Osmetix Ltd have asked for a cash budget to be prepared for the 4 months ending 31 July 2013.

   The following information is available.

   (a)   The company's balance at bank on 1 April 2013 is expected to be £20,000.

   (b)   Sales forecasts are as follows:

February	March	April	May	June	July
£000	£000	£000	£000	£000	£000
160	160	170	170	180	180

   40% of sales are on a cash basis. 50% of credit customers are allowed one month's credit, 10% of credit customers are allowed two months' credit. (Assume credit customers take full advantage of these credit terms.)

(c)   Purchases forecasts are as follows:

March	April	May	June	July
£000	£000	£000	£000	£000
80	100	100	120	120

(d)   All purchases are on credit and are paid for in the month following purchase. Some suppliers offer a 5% cash discount. It is estimated that 50% of all payments to credit suppliers will attract this cash discount.

(e)   The company's expenses will total £20,000 per month. This figure includes depreciation of non-current assets of £4,000 per month.

(f)   In June 2013 a dividend will be paid on ordinary shares. The directors are proposing to pay a dividend of 12p per share. The company has an issued share capital of £500,000 made up of shares with a nominal value of 50p each.

Prepare the company's cash budget for each of the 4 months ending 31 July 2013. (Work in £000s.)

3   In March 2011 Jamal Maharaj opened a retail business selling music technology and computer software. His business has been very successful. He has plans to open a new branch in the near future. A friend has recommended that he ought to prepare budgets to help with his management of his growing business.

Discuss the friend's proposal that Jamal prepares budgets to help with the management of his business.

4   Cozobix Ltd is a company which supplies bathroom fittings and accessories. The following information has been available for the preparation of a cash budget for each of the three months ending October 2013.

(a)   On 1 August 2013 the company's bank balance is expected to be £8,400 overdrawn.

(b)   Sales for June 2013 are forecast to be £200,000. Thereafter sales are expected to increase by 5% comparing one month with the previous month. All sales are on credit with 50% of customers paying one month after sale, and 50% of customers paying two months after sale.

(c)

Forecasts for:	July	August	September	October
	£	£	£	£
Purchases	108,000	121,000	124,000	127,000
Operating expenses (including depreciation charges)	32,300	34,500	35,800	36,100

Purchases are paid for in the month after the purchase takes place.

Operating expenses are paid for in the month they are incurred.

Non-current assets are depreciated by £2,400 per month.

(d)   In August 2013 the directors are proposing to make a one for two rights issue of ordinary shares. The company's current issued share capital consists of 800,000 ordinary shares of 50p each. The shares will be offered at a premium of 20p per share.

(e)   In October 2013 the directors will make a dividend payment of 5p per share on all the ordinary shares in issue at this date.

(f)   The directors are proposing to sell a delivery vehicle for cash in September 2013. The vehicle cost £18,000 when it was purchased on 1 January 2010. The vehicle

AQA Examiner's tip

Take care with the heading for a cash budget. The following points are important:

± inclusion of the name of the business

± clear statement about the time period being covered

± use of the word 'ending' rather than ended, because the budget is for a future period.

± inclusion of £ sign at the top of each column.

has been depreciated at 20% per annum using the straight-line method in the annual financial statements prepared on 31 December each year. No depreciation is provided on non-current assets in the year of their disposal. The directors expect to receive the net book value for the delivery vehicle.

Prepare the company's cash budget for each of the three months ending 31 October 2013.

11 Impact of ICT on accounting

Case study

'Bliss Chocolates'

Ryoma is the owner of a chain of retail outlets based in several shopping centres. These shops sell high-quality chocolates and are called 'Bliss Chocolates'. Ryoma manages the business himself, but he employs shop assistants at each branch.

Nowadays it is very unusual to find anyone keeping financial records manually. Computer technology, and particularly the development of specialised accounting software packages and, of course, spreadsheets, have revolutionised the way in which financial records are kept. In this chapter you will develop an understanding of the immense advantages these technological changes have made to business accounting, but also be able to reflect on some potential drawbacks. You will not be expected to demonstrate any skills in the use of computers or software packages. However, it is likely that, since you have probably used spreadsheets, you will find you are able to understand the contents of this chapter relatively easily. You will learn how to apply your understanding of the advantages and disadvantages of computerisation from various points of view such as that of the owner of the business or the business's employees.

◾ The advantages of computerised accounting records

Why have computerised accounting records?

◾ **Greater accuracy**: computer processes are automatic and are, therefore, error free. Human error is still possible, of course, but this is limited to the potential to make mistakes when inputting information or formulas.

◾ **Greater speed**: computer processes, such as calculating, are virtually instantaneous.

◾ **Simultaneous updating** of records follows from making just one entry.

◾ **Improved accessibility**: it is possible to find information much more quickly.

◾ **More information available**: it is possible to produce specific reports on key aspects of running the business because data can be analysed at great speed.

◾ **Cut in staff costs**: because so much of the work in recording financial information is done automatically, it is possible that fewer staff will be required to keep records, leading to a savings in wages.

Illustration

Bliss Chocolates acquires a computerised accounting system

Ryoma purchased a computer system and appropriate hardware a few years after opening Bliss Chocolates. He found that the change from using manual methods made a great difference to the way he ran his business. With the accounting software, all that was necessary was to just enter the details from source documents such as suppliers' invoices, paying-in slip counterfoils, etc., and detailed accounts were produced automatically. He was also able to produce a range of important reports on his business automatically and at any time he chose, for example:

- trial balance
- detailed list of suppliers, amounts outstanding including an analysis of when each payable was last paid
- financial statements showing profit for the business as a whole
- financial statements showing the turnover and profit and loss at each branch.

As a result he felt he had a much better idea of how his business was performing, and that he was in a much better position to make important decisions. For example, he was able to see week-by-week and month-by-month just how well each retail outlet was performing.

He also used the accounting software to produce:

- payroll records including pay slips for his shop assistants
- inventory control records that would help him make sure products were re-ordered in a timely fashion for any branch of his business
- a non-current asset register providing a comprehensive record of important information about each of the business's non-current assets.

Ryoma found spreadsheets very valuable for preparing cash budgets. He found it was easy to try out a variety of scenarios with the spreadsheet producing new cash budgets instantly. As a result he could keep track of the impact of any changes to his plans for the business, producing more and more variations in budgets until he was satisfied with the results.

He was aware that if he chose to sell on credit, the accounting software would produce sales invoices. He would also be able to generate reports on receivables that would detail how much was outstanding and for how long accounts had been unpaid. He appreciated that these reports could help identify likely bad debts.

Activity

Explain why accounting packages are faster and more accurate than manual accounting methods.

Activity

Explain why spreadsheets are particularly useful for preparing cash budgets.

Disadvantages of computerised accounting systems

What are the disadvantages of having a computerised accounting system?

- *Capital expenditure*: the cost of the equipment and software can be high and the economic life of computer systems can be quite short. It may also be necessary to have software tailored for particular needs and this can also be expensive. Some computer software could have to be updated at frequent intervals.
- *Training costs:* if staff are inexperienced in using software they will need to be trained. When software updates come through, retraining may be necessary. Some staff could find the prospect of training alarming. On the other hand, staff who are skilled in the use of accounting software will be in demand and may be able to command higher salaries. So introducing computerised accounting records could be seen as an opportunity by some employees.
- *Staff morale:* the introduction of computer systems may lead to staff cuts that in turn could affect staff morale.
- *Risk of data loss and security breaches:* computer systems can be vulnerable to 'crashing', viruses and hacking.

Illustration

Bliss Chocolates experiences some disadvantages from having a computerised accounting system

Ryoma's capital expenditure on the computer system was high. He paid for a network of computers, their installation and software in the form of a specialised software package that included payroll and inventory control facilities. He also paid to have the software tailored to his need to produce detailed information about each branch of the business. One of his part-time employees who had maintained the financial records did not feel able to cope with change to computerised records and left the business. This employee was not replaced. The change in staffing unsettled some of the other employees. Ryoma paid for the other finance staff to be trained in the use of the software. Apart from the cost of the training, there was the difficulty of the transition period from manual records to computerised records. Ryoma was advised that it would be wise to keep both systems in operation for a short period during this period of transition. The cost of maintaining the system also proved high. There were a number of occasions he had to call out specialist help when problems arose with operating the system. Ryoma also found that once his staff were trained the risk of losing them increased simply because they had gained marketable skills.

AQA Examiner's tip

In a question requiring an evaluation it is important to focus on both the benefits and drawbacks of the proposal. Check from whose viewpoint you are making an evaluation. Is it the owner of the business, or is it the staff? Remember to give a clear recommendation at the end of your answer with a concise justification.

Activity

Identify two reasons why staff morale might be adversely affected by introducing a computerised accounting system.

Learning outcomes

As a result of studying this chapter, you should now be able to:

- explain the advantages and disadvantages of computerisation in regard to accounting and financial record keeping
- explain some specific computer applications that benefit businesses
- assess the impact of computerisation of accounting functions from the viewpoint of the owner of the business and from the viewpoint of employees

AQA Examination Style Questions

1   For some years Carol Marshall has used a basic computer system for keeping her wholesale business's accounting records. She is now proposing to upgrade the system and purchase new software which can be used in connection with her inventory records and sales ledger. Explain the specific benefits which the upgrade could potentially provide for her (i) her inventory records and (ii) sales ledger.

2   The finance director of Tinterell Ltd is proposing to overhaul the way accounting records are prepared for the company. Currently the staff use a mixture of manual records and computerised records using rather dated software

Prepare a report to the finance director in (i) explaining why the accounts staff may be concerned about this proposal, and (ii) explaining reasons which might persuade the accounts staff that the proposal will be beneficial to them.

Examination skills

Probably almost all of us have sat down at some time in an examination room, opened the exam paper and had some kind of bad experience, for example:

■ 'I cannot remember how to do a question on that topic'

■ 'I don't really know what I was supposed to do to answer that question'

■ 'I don't think I have read the question carefully enough'

■ 'I am going to run out of time'

Having worked hard through your course of study, you will, of course, be anxious to avoid any of these problems. There are probably two key things that could really help you do well and perhaps better than you might expect: being well prepared, of course, and gaining a good understanding of how the examination works.

■ Preparation during your course of study

Getting organised

Do you keep your homework answers, class handouts, model answers and class notes carefully? Could you find an answer to a question on a key topic easily? Could you find a model answer to that same question? The point of these questions is that when it comes to preparing for a test or for the final examination, you will need to be able to find these documents easily so that you get on to the task of revising without wasting any time.

Study skills

As well as working on all the new accounting topics and answering questions, have you also given some thought to how you learn best? For example, some students find it difficult to remember the correct order for shares and reserves on a company's statement of financial position. Have you developed any memorising techniques that work for you and enable you to recall factual information relatively easily? Many students make up a memorable phrase or saying to help them with this sort of task. How about 'Oliver (ordinary shares) plays (preference shares) chess (capital reserves) regularly (revenue reserves)' as an example. Well, this phrase may not be memorable for you, but make up another alternative one and make it as silly as you like!

The idea of mnemonics, as illustrated in the previous paragraph, is probably familiar to you. But what about these other ideas . . .?

Marking your own work:

Do you regularly mark your own work against a model answer or the mark scheme provided by AQA, or do you pair up with someone else and mark each other's work? If you carry out this activity regularly then you are likely to get to really understand how you can earn marks in the examination, but more than that you can focus your attention on what you did well, but also, of course, on what went wrong. There is much research to show that students who regularly 'self-assess' (mark your own work) or 'peer assess' (pair up with someone and mark each other's work) significantly improve their performance in the subjects they are studying.

'Repairing' your answers:

Assuming you, or someone else, has just marked some work you have done, do you take a little time to focus on what went wrong? Again there is considerable evidence that students who regularly take a careful look at any part of an answer that went wrong and take some actions make substantial progress, often well beyond the progress that the individual expects can be made. The idea here is that you use a model answer to help you understand what you should have done when some part of a computational answer is incorrect. Take the trouble to write out a note on your marked work about what you should have done using the evidence in the model answer, and ensure that you understand how the model answer was achieved (perhaps with the help of the teacher or a fellow student). By the way, don't worry about making your piece of work look a bit messy! The ideal would be if you could say to yourself 'if I did this question again, I am confident I could get those difficult bits right'. Then, what about prose answers. Most students of accounting find prose answers rather difficult to do well. Again, use this idea of 'repairing' answers to help you make progress. In the case of a prose answer, this means noting on your own piece of work points made in the model answer that you omitted, or did not express very well. You will need to do this regularly throughout the course, but once again the evidence is that students who get into the habit of regularly using model answers in this way make considerable progress and over time begin to build up real confidence in preparing prose answers based on a good understanding of the points that they should include.

Monitoring your own progress

Many of you who are studying accounting in a school or college will have been provided with information about how well you should perform in this subject based on your performance in GCSEs. Perhaps you have been given information so that you work this out for yourself, or perhaps you have just been given what is often called a target grade. You could well, of course, have decided what level of performance you wish to obtain any way, never mind the target grade set by someone else. The question is: do you regularly monitor your own performance against one or all of these targets? Perhaps you do this in discussions with your tutor or subject teacher. Regularly checking on how well you are doing against your expectations can be valuable in helping you maintain the level of progress you need to make.

Examination practice

Have you tried plenty of past examination questions? If you are to be thoroughly prepared for the examination you do need to make sure you have tried past questions on every key topic in the examination. Have you given enough attention to both computational and prose questions? Don't forget the balance; there will be a fair proportion of both types of question in the examination for both AS modules. You will also find it helpful to ensure you answer these questions fully and with great attention to matters of presentation. For example, make a point of using proper headings for financial statements and don't get into the habit of cutting corners to save time. You need to go into the exam not having to think too hard about how best to present answers; this should be second nature to you at this stage.

Revising for the examinations

As the examination for each unit draws near you will be thinking about the best way to revise. Just how much revision is done and how frequently it is done will, of course, vary from one student to another. In accounting it is important that a substantial amount of your revision time is spent actually answering questions, so that you ensure you are skilled in actually carrying out accounting techniques, or that you remember key points to make in a variety of questions requiring a prose response. You might find it useful to make a checklist of all the main topics in each of the AS modules and work your way through the list finding questions to try on each item. If you have organised your work carefully you should be able to find a relevant question, an answer that you have produced yourself, a model answer or the exam mark scheme for each item on your checklist. If you feel confident about a topic just try the trickier parts of the question again, avoiding looking at the model answer unless you really get stuck. There is no need to produce carefully presented answers at this stage, unless you really want to; you will probably be more concerned to make the best use of your precious revision time, so for once cut corners, and perhaps produce key points for questions requiring a prose response rather than full answers. If you are less sure about a topic, be prepared to spend more time on it. Try working through the entire question, rather than just selected elements. Again, have a model answer around to help you when you get stuck. In the end you will find that actually answering questions will help you recover all the skills you had developed far more quickly than just looking through your notes and looking at your answers to past questions.

How the examination works

If you understand how the examination works it is very unlikely you will experience any surprises when you actually sit down to do the exam.

The structure of the examination paper

The following table sets out some key points about each of the two AS module assessment units (i.e. examinations). You will see that the papers have almost identical structures.

Questions about the structure of the examination	Unit 1	Unit 2
How long is the exam?	1 hour 30 minutes	1 hour 30 minutes
How many questions will I have to answer?	Four compulsory questions	Four compulsory questions
Will there be a choice of questions?	No	No
Will each question carry equal marks?	No, the questions will be of varying length and have varying numbers of tasks	No, the questions will be of varying length and have varying numbers of tasks
How many marks on each paper?	80	80
What is the likely balance between questions requiring a computational response and those requiring a prose response?	Approximately 60 marks for 'computational' questions and 20 marks for 'prose' questions	Approximately 55 marks for 'computational' questions and 25 marks for 'prose' questions

What are the examiners trying to assess?

Examination papers are designed with great care to ensure that candidates have an opportunity to show what they can do. You will find that papers try to cover as much of the subject content in one paper as possible, for example. However, it would be almost impossible to write an examination paper that included tasks on every aspect of the specification. Over several papers, though, the aim will be to examine every part of the specification. You will find that the tasks for each question are designed to include some that most candidates are likely to find easy. Wherever possible, the examiner will try to start the paper off with a more straightforward question so that candidates have a chance to make a good start and settle their nerves a little. It is likely that the last tasks in a particular question will be harder for most candidates. The examiner will be keen to make sure that candidates who are likely to achieve a lower grade have a good opportunity to demonstrate some knowledge, understanding and skills, but will also be keen to include tasks which only the candidates who will achieve the higher grades are likely to be able to do well.

It will not be apparent to most candidates looking at the examination paper that the examiner has also tried to ask questions that test important 'educational' skills:

- **knowledge and understanding** – meaning can you define terms, explain accounting techniques, ideas and concepts; do you know how to set out accounting statements, etc.
- **application** – meaning can you demonstrate skill in applying what you know about accounting techniques and prepare financial records and statements for a particular business, etc.
- **analysis and evaluation** – can you select information, organise the information in a useful way, draw conclusions from the information, explain your conclusions to others and produce a balanced argument about the strengths and weaknesses of a particular situation or process?

A general awareness of these types of questions will help you prepare effectively for the examination. Broadly speaking, almost all candidates can usually do quite well in regard to 'knowledge and understanding'; fewer candidates are as confident when it comes to applying the knowledge, understanding and skills, and fewer still do well at analysis and evaluation questions. Do bear this in mind, particularly if you are aiming for a high grade.

In the two AS module assessment units the balance of questions that test these skills is as follows:

Skill	Unit 1	Unit 2
Knowledge and understanding	40%	20%
Application	50%	50%
Analysis and evaluation	10%	30%

Getting the timing right

Examination papers are written so that candidates should be able to complete all the questions in the time allowed. Of course, part of the skill of accounting is being able to process data quickly, so that there is an expectation that candidates should not have to take an undue amount of time trying to take in all the information provided. If you have taken examination practice seriously, you will have got used to getting on with the tasks as soon as you can. All candidates, however, do need to make sure they are making best use of the time available. It would be very damaging to your overall result if you mistimed things so badly that, for example, you failed to answer one of the questions. Clearly, in these circumstances your potential mark will be scaled down considerably.

It is often a good idea to divide up the 90 minutes available to complete the exam between the questions in roughly the proportion of the marks available. Don't take too long over working this out in the exam room, of course; an approximate calculation will probably do. Here are two examples to show you how this could work.

Example 1:

Marks available for each question	Calculation	Time available for each question (approximately)
20	There are 80 marks on the paper and 90 minutes to complete the paper; so you need to score 1 mark every 1.125 minutes	22
24		26
10		11
26		30
80 marks	TOTAL MARKS AND TIME	90 minutes

Example 2:

Marks available for each question	Calculation	Time available for each question (approximately)
15	There are 80 marks on the paper and 90 minutes to complete the paper; so you need to score 1 mark every 1.125 minutes	17
23		25
31		36
11		12
80 marks	TOTAL MARKS AND TIME	90 minutes

With approximate timing worked out, try to keep with the time for each question as you write your answers. Remember that every time you exceed the time you have allocated you will have to speed up in another question to make up the time lost.

If things get a little desperate, despite all this careful planning, don't give up! Do your best to find ways of showing that you can demonstrate you have a good understanding of the task(s) that you think you may have to rush through. If they are tasks requiring a prose response, perhaps abandon writing full

statements and offer the main points in a bulleted list. You will not score full marks for this type of answer, but you will gain credit for the amount of knowledge and understanding you are showing.

Key words in questions

Examiners use a number of words when setting questions such as 'state', 'explain', 'discuss'. The examiner has an expectation that each of these types of word will produce a particular kind of answer. Obviously, it is important for candidates to understand exactly what the examiner's expectations are. Look through the following list of key words used in examination questions in accounting.

You probably don't need reminding of the most common problem in examinations, i.e. the candidate did not read the question properly and so did not produce the required answer. Again, practice will help you get the balance of time spent reading questions carefully to actually answering the questions in the right proportion. So when the question says 'prepare a statement of financial position (balance sheet) extract showing . . .', spend enough time reading the question to note the word extract, otherwise, of course, you could end up wasting a lot of time producing a complete statement of financial position (balance sheet)!

Key term	What the examiner expects	Examples
Identify / State	This type of question usually tests factual recall. You are not expected to write at length; just one word or a phrase will usually be sufficient.	Q: Identify the accounting concept that is used when valuing stocks A: Just one word required. i.e. 'prudence'
List	Again this type of question is concerned with factual recall and a few words at most are all that is usually expected.	Q: List three concepts that are used when valuing assets A: Again just words or phrases required, i.e. 'objectivity, cost, going concern'
Explain	This question is testing how much you really understand and so more is expected by the examiner. You will need to write several sentences at least. In one sentence you will need to convey that you have a basic understanding of the subject matter of the question. It will then be important to develop this answer further to score full marks. You will need, therefore, to add other statements in which you show that you have a good grasp of the background to the subject matter of the topic, that you can illustrate the points you have made, perhaps providing examples.	Q: Explain the accounting concept of consistency. A: Here several sentences required each demonstrating various degrees of understanding. The concept consistency requires businesses to use the same accounting methods and policies from one accounting period to the next (basic idea). This will ensure that valid comparisons can be made of one year's results with those for another year (showing further understanding). The user of accounts will, therefore, be able to make valid judgements and decisions based on the comparison (showing yet more understanding). For example, if a business adopts the straight-line method of depreciation, this method should be applied in each accounting period (providing an illustration or example that provides further evidence of understanding).

Prepare	This question will usually require accounting statements to be produced. This type of question is designed to test your knowledge of the correct layouts for various financial statements, your ability to work through the statements in the correct sequence and to select data, sometimes making calculations, from that provided. The setting for the question (i.e. the business that is the subject of the question) and occasionally the way some of the data is presented will be unfamiliar to you.	Q: Prepare a cash budget A: You will produce a cash budget using a conventional layout. Sometimes a template may be given
Calculate	This question will require you to select the correct data and use the correct arithmetical processes to produce a particular result. The question is likely to test your understanding of a particular accounting technique.	Q: Calculate the gearing ratio A: You will need to state the formula for this ratio; select the correct figures from all the data supplied; correctly divide (in this case) fixed-return finance by all finance, and finally present your answer in the correct form, i.e. a percentage
Discuss	This type of question requires you to demonstrate a full understanding of a topic by presenting arguments that either support or counter a particular course of action. You will be expected to give your final view and provide a justification for your view based on the arguments you have outlined.	Q: Discuss whether a sole trader should convert the business into a partnership A: Your answer should present the case for staying as a sole trader (i.e. an explanation of the benefits of being a sole trader) and the disadvantages of this type of business organisation. The answer should then explain the extent to which forming a partnership would overcome any of the difficulties of being a sole trader, and the extent to which being in partnership might produce new disadvantages. Your answer should end with a final judgement based on the arguments you have presented and include a concise justification for the view you have taken
Evaluate	This type of question requires you to weigh up the strengths and weaknesses of a particular accounting process or technique, or a particular course of action, or the performance of a business. You are expected to reach a final overall judgement, perhaps in the form of a recommendation or piece of advice. Your final judgement should be accompanied by a concise justification for your view.	Q: Evaluate a sole trader's decision to introduce a system of budgetary control A: Your answer will include an explanation of the benefits of introducing budgetary control. The best answers would include illustrations relevant to the particular business being considered. You should then provide an explanation of the possible disadvantages of budgetary control. Again include illustrations that relate to the business under consideration. Finally, you should express your overall view as to whether budgetary control should be introduced and provide a short justification

Getting the finer details right

If you look back through Chapters 1 to 11 you will recall that examiner tips have been included to help you produce the best answers possible in examinations. Many of these tips relate to particular topics, but here are some of the points made that might apply to a wide range of questions.

■ Provide correct headings for all financial statements and avoid using any abbreviations in the titles such as y/e, 31 Dec 10, etc. In

addition, do make a point of naming the business concerned.

Examples of good practice:

Income statement for the year ended 31 December 2007

Statement of financial position at 30 September 2010

Cash budget for each of the four months ending 30 November 2010

Provide workings to support the figures you use in answers to computation tasks. Unless the calculation is very straightforward, the person marking your script will need to know, step by step, how you reached your final figure. As you probably already know, there are often marks for each step in a calculating process, and without the evidence these marks may be not be allocated to you.

Examples of good practice:

Proposed ordinary shared dividend   £12,500

[5% × 500,000 shares of 50p each

= 5% × £250,000]

Depreciation of equipment

[30% × net book value (cost £40,000 less

existing depreciation £12,000)

= 30% × £28,000]   £8,400

Take some trouble to use the right technical terms in prose answers and the correct labels for subtotals in financial statements. If you have the knowledge and understanding don't hesitate to show off!

Examples of good practice:

In a company's income statement

Profit before tax

Depreciation is based on an assessment of the *economic life* of a non-current asset

(rather than 'depreciation is based on an estimate of how long the non-current asset will last')

In each examination four of the marks will be allocated to what is called the 'quality of written communication'. The person who marks your script will be looking for some particular points when awarding these marks:

Spelling: is your spelling generally good? It does not have to be perfect! Anyone can misspell a word, particularly under the pressure of completing an examination.

Punctuation: have you followed the usual conventions in regard to the use of punctuation?

Grammar: have you written in sentences and are these grammatically correct? Avoid a list of bulleted points in prose answers (except when you are really under pressure to complete a task). Again the odd slip-up will be considered acceptable.

Presentation: have you used conventional layouts for accounting statements, including reports and memoranda, and have you provided accurate headings, subheadings, etc?

Terminology: in prose answers have you used terms correctly and avoided using everyday language when there are specific words or phrases which are part of the language of accounting?

Glossary

'DEAD CLIC': a mnemonic to help remember the rules of Dr and Cr: **D**ebit, **E**xpenditure, **A**ssets, **D**rawings, **C**redit, **L**iabilities, **I**ncome, **C**apital.

A

Accruals: expenses and revenues are matched for a time period when calculating profit.

Annual general meeting: often called the AGM is the yearly company meeting that can be attended by shareholders.

Assets: resources that are available for use by the business.

Auditors' fees: the amount paid to those who check the accounting records. This item is an expense.

Authorised capital: the maximum amount of capital the company can issue by way of shares.

B

Bad debt recovered: an amount received from a receivable that has previously been written off.

Bad debt written off: amount owed by a receivables that is irrecoverable.

Balancing off accounts: the process of calculating the balance between the debits and credits on a ledger account and carrying forward the balance into the next accounting period.

Bank overdraft: a form of loan where the bank allows a customer to be overdrawn (make total payments in excess of total receipts) up to a specified limit.

Bank statement: a printout issued by the bank detailing all receipts into the account, payments out of the account and a running balance.

Bonus issue: the issue of additional shares to shareholders in proportion to their existing shareholders. No cash is paid for the additional shares. The issue is financed from company reserves, resulting in a re-structuring of the capital and reserves section of the statement of financial position.

Business entity concept: an accounting system contains records of that organisation only.

C

Cancelled cheque: a cheque drawn by the business and subsequently cancelled before payment.

Capital: resources (cash or other assets) introduced by the owner to run the business.

Capital employed: for a limited company this is made up of shares + reserves + non-current liabilities.

Capital expenditure: money spent on non-current assets that is intended to benefit future financial periods.

Capital reserve: profits that have been set aside and do not originate from the everyday trading activities of the company. Capital reserves cannot be distributed as dividends.

Cash book: book of original entry recording cash and cheque payments and receipts. The cash book also has columns to record discount received and discount allowed.

Cash budget: a plan showing estimated future receipts and payments that enables possible surpluses or shortages of cash to be identified.

Cash discount: a reduction in the amount owing to a supplier in return for settling their bills early (e.g. payment within 14 days).

Cash receipts and till rolls: contains details of cash received.

Cheque counterfoil: contains details of cheques drawn (date, payee and amount).

Consistency concept: accounting methods are applied in the same way in each accounting period.

Contra entry: in a cash book the records of funds transferred from the cash account to the bank account and vice-versa.

Contra: an amount set off in the sales ledger account against the purchases ledger account of the same person(s) and vice-versa.

Control: in budgeting, the idea of setting limits to expenditure so that the business as a whole will function well.

Co-ordination: in budgeting, the idea of bringing together a range of factors when determining the timing of events.

Corporation tax: tax on a company's profits.

Cost concept: the price paid for the asset.

Cost of sales: total purchases plus carriage inwards and returnsoutwards adjusted for opening and closing inventory on hand.

Credit note: a document detailing sales or purchase returns or an overcharge, together with reasons.

Current assets: company resources that are planned to be converted into cash within 12 months.

Current liabilities: monies owed by the business due for repayment within twelve months.

D

Debentures: loans to a company on which a fixed rate of interest is paid. The interest is an expense to be charged to the profit and loss account.

Delivery note: a document detailing the goods that have been delivered by the supplier.

Depreciation: the loss in value of a non-current asset over its useful economic life that is apportioned to financial periods. It is a non-cash expense.

Direct debit: where authority is granted by the business to a third party for fixed or variable payments to be made at the request of that third party.

Directors: the senior managers of a limited company; appointed by shareholders at the AGM.

Directors' fees: the amount paid for the work done by directors. This item is an expense.

Discount allowed: discount given to customers who settle bills promptly.

Discount received: discount received from suppliers for settling our bills promptly.

Drawings: funds withdrawn from the business by the owner for personal use.

E

Equity: the shares and reserves of a limited company.

Equity shares: are ordinary shares.

Estimated residual value: the estimated value of the asset at the end of its useful life.

Estimated useful economic life: the estimated time that the business will continue to use the asset.

F

Finance charges: include interest on loans and preferences share dividends paid.

Financial statements: the income statement and statement of financial position (balance sheet) (sometimes called final accounts).

G

Gearing: is fixed-return financing (preference shares and long-term liabilities) in relation to all sources of finance (shares, reserves and non-current liabilities); the ratio is expressed as a percentage.

General journal: book of original entry recording non-routine transactions that do not appear in the other books of original entry.

General ledger: a ledger containing all impersonal accounts.

Going concern concept: the assumption that a business will continue to trade for the foreseeable future.

Gross profit margin: gross profit in relation to revenue (measured as a percentage).

Gross profit: the difference between revenue and the cost of sales.

I

Income due: money that should have been received by a business from a receivable (such as a tenant) relating to the current financial period but that is yet to be received.

Income received in advance: money received by a business from a receivable (such as a tenant) but that relates to the next financial period.

Income statement: a financial statement used to calculate a businesses profit and loss.

Interim dividend: a half-yearly dividend payment.

Inventory: stocks of goods for resale.

Invoice: a document detailing the goods or services supplied and the price paid.

Issued capital: the amount of shares that the company has chosen to issue to date.

L

Liabilities: monies owed by the business.

Limited liability company: a form of organisation whose owners (or members) own shares and where the owners enjoy the benefit of having limited liability for the debts of the business. Companies have a separate existence from their owners.

Limited liability: the responsibility of the owners of the business (shareholders) for the debts of the business is limited to the amount they have agreed to invest.

Liquid capital ratio: is liquid capital in relation to current liabilities; the ratio is sometimes called the acid test ratio. This is an important measure of liquidity.

Liquid capital: is current assets excluding inventories.

Liquidity: the ability of a business to access sufficient cash resources to pay its short-term liabilities.

Loss: the final figure in the income statement when the gross profit is *less than* the expenses that have been deducted from it.

M

Mark-up: gross profit in relation to cost of sales (measured as a percentage).

Materiality concept: if the amount involved is relatively insignificant, then the usual accounting treatment of an item can be set aside.

Monitoring: in budgeting, the idea of comparing what actually happens with what has been forecast and investigating why differences occur.

Mortgage: a long-term loan, usually secured against assets.

N

Net cost: initial cost of the asset less the estimated residual value at the end of the asset's useful economic life.

Net current assets/liabilities: the difference between current assets and current liabilities.

Net current assets ratio: is current assets in relation to current liabilities; the ratio is sometimes called the current ratio or the working capital ratio. This is an important measure of liquidity.

Net realisable value: sale value less any costs necessary to incur a sale.

Nominal accounts: a type of impersonal account relating to all non-real accounts.

Non-current assets: resources owned by the business intended for continuing use in running the business rather than for resale.

Non-current liabilities: monies owed by the business due for repayment at a time after 12 months.

O

Objectivity concept: factual information is preferred because it is likely to be beyond dispute.

Operating profit: profit before finance charges and tax.

Order of liquidity: the order in which current assets are able to be turned into cash.

Ordinary shares: shares that carry voting rights and have a variable dividend that is dependent on the amount of profits.

Outstanding (uncleared) lodgements: bank deposits that have been recorded in the cash book but have not yet been processed by the bank.

Overhead to revenue: each overhead in relation to revenue (measured as a percentage).

P

Partnership: where two or more individuals run a continuing business for profit.

Par value; nominal value: the face value of a share.

Payable days: is trade payables in relation to credit purchases; the ratio is expressed as so many days.

Paying in slip counterfoil: contains details on funds paid into the bank (date, source and amount).

Planning: in budgeting, the idea of using objectives and targets as the basis for determining what should happen.

Preference shares: shares that have a fixed rate of dividend and normally have no voting rights.

Private company: one in which only the founders of the company, their family, friends and employees can invest in shares.

Profit: the final figure on the profit and loss account when the gross profit is *greater than* the expenses that have been deducted from it.

Profit after taxation: profit for the year less the provision for corporation tax.

Profit margin: profit in relation to revenue (measured as a percentage).

Provision for doubtful debts: an amount set aside from profits to take account of the likelihood that some receivables will not be able to pay the amount due.

Prudence: where there is doubt, asset and profit values are under- rather than overstated, never assume profit until realised, but

losses should be dealt with when anticipated.

Public company: one in which any member of the public can invest as shares are floated on the open market.

Purchases day book: book of original entry recording credit purchase invoices.

Purchases ledger: a ledger containing individual personal accounts for each credit supplier and recording all transactions with that supplier.

Purchase order: a document used to place an order with a supplier.

Purchases returns day book: book of original entry recording purchase credit notes.

R

Rate of inventory turnover: cost of sales divided by average stock.

Real accounts: a type of impersonal account relating to fixed assets.

Realisable value: sale value.

Realisation concept: revenue should not be recorded in the accounts until it is realised, i.e. when there is cash or the promise of cash.

Receivable days: trade receivables in relation to credit sales; the ratio is expressed as so many days.

Reducing balance method: where the annual depreciation charge is based on the net book value of the non-current asset at the beginning of each financial period.

Remittance advice: a document sent with a payment, advising the recipient which invoices etc., are being paid.

Retained earnings for the year: the amount of profit for the year that has not been distributed by the directors.

Return on capital employed: profit in relation to capital invested (sole trader) or capital employed (limited company), expressed as a percentage. This is an important measure of profitability.

Returned cheque: a cheque that has been paid into the bank, but not honoured by the drawer's

bank (usually because of lack of funds).

Revaluation reserve: arises from the increase in value of a non-current asset above its net book value at the date of the revaluation. The reserve is a capital reserve and may not be used to finance the payment of cash dividends.

Revenue: the total value of sales as recorded in an income statement.

Revenue expenditure: money spent on running costs that benefits only the current financial period.

Revenue reserves: profits that arise from everyday trading activities and that can be distributed as dividends.

Rights issue: an issue of shares for cash where the existing shareholders are offered the right to buy the shares usually at a price below market price.

S

Sales day book: book of original entry recording credit sales invoices.

Sales ledger: a ledger containing individual personal accounts for each credit customer and recording all transactions with that customer.

Sales returns day book: book of original entry recording sales credit notes.

Share premium: the amount paid for a share above its face value.

Shareholders: the owners of a limited liability company.

Shareholders' funds: the total of issued capital and all reserves.

Sole trader: a business owned by one individual. The individual bears sole responsibility for the business's actions.

Stakeholders: individuals, groups or organisations that have an interest in a business or are affected by the business. For example, employees, customers, suppliers, owners, investors, etc.

Standing order: where a fixed payment is made at regular intervals by the bank on the instructions of the business.

Statement of account: a document sent to a customer detailing all recent transactions and informing them of the total amount outstanding.

Statement of Changes in Equity: forms part of the financial statements of a limited liability company. It provides details of each element of issued capital and each reserve and the changes that have occured to the opening figures for these items during the course of a financial year.

Statement of financial position (Balance sheet): a statement detailing all of the assets and liabilities of a business.

Straight-line method: where the annual depreciation charge is based on the cost of the non-current asset.

Suspense account: a temporary account used to post a difference in the trial balance (i.e. the total of the debit side does not equal the total of the credit side) until such time as the differences are identified.

T

Trade discount: offered to businesses in a similar line of business, as distinct from the general public, often as an incentive for buying in bulk quantities.

Trade payables: amounts owing to suppliers.

Trade receivables: amounts owed by customers.

True and fair view: the principle that accounting records should be factually accurate wherever possible, or otherwise present a reasonable estimate of, or judgment about, the financial position.

Turnover: sales net of returns in.

U

Unlimited liability: the owner of a business is fully responsible for all the debts of the business.

Unpresented cheques: cheques that have been drawn and entered in the cash book, but have not yet been presented to the bank for payment.

Index